IGNITE YOUR PASSION FOR GOD

A Daily Guide to Experiencing Personal Revival

TOM PHILLIPS
WITH
LISA MARZANO

MOODY PRESS
CHICAGO

Library of Congress Cataloging-in-Publication Data

Phillips, Tom, 1947-
    Ignite your passion for God : a daily guide for experiencing God's personal
renewal / Tom Phillips with Lisa Marzano.
        p. cm.
    Includes bibliographical references.
    ISBN 0-8024-5248-5
    1. Spiritual life—Christianity. 2. Christian life. I. Phillips, Tom. II. Title.

BV4501.2 .P532 2001
248.4—dc21

00-063808

1 3 5 7 9 10 8 6 4 2

Printed in the United States of America

CONTENTS

to my parents,
John T. and Lorene Phillips,
who taught me that God can accomplish anything that He wants
through obedient servants.
Through their example I have seen individuals who sought,
in the midst of a very real world,
intimacy with Christ,
thus they showed to me a visualization of the real, real world.
TOM PHILLIPS

to Kathy Maas,
whose friendship has been a resting place for a weary traveler.
I love you, my friend.
LISA MARZANO

FOREWORD

On July 5, 1994, I felt God lead me to begin a forty-day fast for two purposes. The first was to pray on behalf of a great spiritual revival and awakening in America and the world. The second was to fast and pray for the fulfillment of the Great Commission throughout the world. Though I have been committed to these two purposes since my conversion to Christ in 1945, I have recently sensed a special urgency.

As believers in Christ, we are at war with the enemy of our souls, and I think it is a matter of life and death to hundred of millions that we be faithful to our Lord and fight the battle for the souls of men like never before in history. Unprecedented opportunities to help fulfill the Great Commission are now open to us.

The world in which we live is rapidly changing into a place where suicide, drug addiction and murder are the norm, and being part of a normal nuclear family is unusual. Americans are selfish and cynical, and the church—the body of Christ—often seems asleep. *Ignite Your Passion for God* is a call for the church to wake up to revival, one heart at a time.

We cannot ask God for too much as it relates to the fulfillment of the Great Commission if our hearts and motives are pure, and we do everything according to His Word and His will and for His glory.

Still, there are human hindrances that can stand in the way of fulfilling these goals, including pride, lack of faith, mediocrity, and carnality. There is no place for

FOREWORD

such attitudes. In the front lines of battle, soldiers know that their very lives depend on unity and cooperation as they support their follow soldiers.

In this book, Tom Phillips encourages the church to stop waiting for God to pour out revival and to aggressively become a vehicle through which God can do that very thing. Revival begins in our hearts as we say, "Spirit of God, breathe on me. I'll be obedient. I'll walk in faith. I'll fast. I'll pray. I'll share your Word with all you put in my path." As we take these steps, we will become vessels God can use to help bring revival to believers and an awakening to seekers after truth—an awakening to those around us, to our country, and to the world.

Ultimately, if we are going to see the world reached for Christ, you and I must die to self (Galatians 2:20), a biblical truth Tom emphasizes in this book.

I appreciate the heart Tom has carried for revival for so many years. He shares his heart in this guidebook, and if you listen carefully, you'll learn and grow. It's time to change the world through personal revival. I stand on tiptoe with anticipation to see what God is going to do in and through His church and in and through you and me.

Bill Bright, Founder and President
Campus Crusade for Christ

ACKNOWLEDGMENTS

The first individual who stirred the spark of and for revival that God had placed in me prior to my birth is Lewis Drummond, Billy Graham Chair of Evangelism and professor at Beeson Seminary, and previous president of Southeastern Baptist Seminary. "Dr. D," who also served as the Billy Graham Chair of Evangelism at Southern Baptist Theological Seminary in Louisville, Kentucky, literally pointed me toward my destiny. My vision for revival and for this book is largely a result of his passion.

My thanks also to Charlie Riggs, the director of counseling and follow-up for the Billy Graham Evangelistic Association for almost forty years and my spiritual mentor. He has shown me through his teachings in the preparation for Billy Graham Crusades as well as his life that there is the possibility of personal revival on a daily basis—and corporately through the church—when people are pure before the Lord through conviction, repentance, confession, and seeking Jesus Christ as one's most intimate relationship. Thank you, Dr. Riggs—and Dr. Drummond, too—for all that you have meant to the kingdom of God, and to one servant boy from Mississippi.

My thanks to Terry Whalin as he worked with me on the initial book proposal and Lisa Marzano and Paulette Shepard as they worked diligently to finalize the many drafts of this book. Lisa, thank you especially for the way in which you have thrown yourself into this work and shared in the heartfelt experiences that led to revival in the final compilation.

ACKNOWLEDGMENTS

My deepest thanks to Billy Graham with whom I had the privilege of serving many years. Though he would say he is solely an evangelist, his heart for revival in ministry of the Word in proclamation has laid the foundation in many ways for the seminal movement of the Spirit of God that we are presently seeing.

Thanks as well to Jim Bell and Moody Press who believe in me enough to offer this opportunity of writing *Ignite Your Passion for God*. Much gratitude goes to Jim Vincent. Your editorial assistance has been invaluable.

Finally, the person who has inspired me most of all in the writing of this work has been my wonderful wife, Ouida, who has given us three children who love Jesus Christ—Cara, Molly, and Matt. I am grateful to them and their spouses, Matt Brown, Madison Morris, and Allison Phillips, respectively, for their endearing support.

Introduction

THE
TIME
IS
NOW

Everywhere you turn the news looks bad. The national and international news are filled with reports of violence. Countries are at war. Millions of children are abused while others starve to death daily. Senseless crimes have stunned many at the end of the twentieth century: A gunman rushes through the security gates of the capitol in Washington, D.C., whips out a gun, and kills two policemen. Two high school students in Colorado kill thirteen others and then themselves. A six-year-old boy in Michigan shoots and kills his six-year-old classmate. Terrorists from London to Libya threaten and kill for their cause. Throughout the world, hate erupts in every urban and rural setting.

Some people choose not to read newspapers or magazines or listen to the nightly news. They wave it off, proclaiming, "It's all bad. What's the point?"

Perhaps it's a matter of perspective. You can see those events from your view as a human, or from God's view. I read the news with extreme interest as I desire to see world events from God's perspective. My prayer for the last twelve years has been from 1 Chronicles 12:32, to be like the people in the tribe of Issachar who "had understanding of the times, to know what Israel ought to do." I've prayed and asked God to help me be a person who understands the times, to see through His eyes what He is doing, and then to know how to respond during a particular *"chairos"* moment in time.

A *chairos* moment is a special moment in time that is predetermined in history.

The Greek word appears only a few times in the Bible; it's not the normal Greek word for time, *chronos*, from which we derive "chronology" or "time."

One of the places Scripture uses *chairos* is in the word "preappointed" in Acts 17:26–28, which states, "And hath made of one blood all nations of men for to dwell on all the face of the earth, and hath determined the times before appointed, and the bounds of their habitation; that they should seek the Lord, if haply they might feel after him, and find him, though he be not far from every one of us: For in him we live, and move, and have our being; as certain also of your own poets have said, For we are also his offspring."

The Lord of the universe used this concept of *chairos* to indicate a special moment, and today in history our world stands in such a time—a time when our world looks incredibly dark. We wonder, "Where is the Good News?" A bit of God's purpose is revealed in this passage in Acts—that we should seek the Lord, feel after *Him*, and find *Him*. Those words mean that we have an obligation and responsibility as Christians to grow in our intimacy with Christ.

Why? Because, as the Scripture notes, it is in Him that we live, move, and have our being. Our life and breath are based on our relationship with God—intimacy with the Creator through Jesus Christ. It is only through this intimacy with God that we can move out and effect change in our world. Revival begins in the single heart of each person.

A *chairos* moment may have begun, or is about to begin, in your own life. Henry Blackaby, coauthor of *Experiencing God*, wrote that people should determine where God is working and jump in the middle of it.[1] Dark events are taking place on earth, but perhaps God is working in the midst of them. If you and I turn our attention and focus on the eternal relationship with God, we will see how He is working personally in our hearts and calling us to open the door for revival in our communities, our country, and the world. He is beginning a worldwide awakening to revival, one person at a time. This workbook can lead you and other participants into refreshing and personal revival, drawing you into greater intimacy with the Father.

A number of books emphasize personal spiritual revival. This workbook is designed with an interactive portion for you to personalize sections and apply them to your daily life. If you choose to take advantage of this *chairos* moment and seek personal revival through this study, I urge you to be kind to yourself and understand that changing some lifetime habits will not occur overnight. The journey toward igniting your passion for God is a process that takes commitment, careful thought, reflective meditation, and action. The workbook section of this book will help you take a more deliberate and process-oriented approach to change. The pilgrimage throughout the meditations in this book should impact your life and transfer into action; otherwise this would be only an intellectual exercise.

While this guide can be used for individual study, it is ideally designed for study within the context of a small group. Being part of a small group will provide some essential elements: accountability, discipline, and authenticity. You and I need to gather around us people whom we trust for their love and encouragement.

Before you begin this practical study, here are some steps to consider:

Prepare. The questions on these pages will help you respond to the day's reading or encourage you to turn to a specific Bible passage. Don't pass over them; read them.

Probe for honest answers to issues. A key ingredient of reflection is looking deeply. Remove any masks or self-doubt and look deeply inside yourself.

Seek the guidance of the Holy Spirit. As you work through this material, try to balance between the structure of the questions and spontaneity. Give yourself permission not to answer every question or follow every assignment. (But don't skip an entire sequence just because it challenges you!) Each reader and each group has a differ-ent set of circumstances and dynamics. If you're in a group, expect some questions to stir intense discussion and interest while others will not be relevant. The group should move through the workbook at a pace comfortable for the group as a whole. If you're working individually, however, give yourself permission to move through the workbook at your own pace. At the same time, seek God's guidance through His Holy Spirit as you work through each section. Remember Jesus' promise: "He, the Spirit of truth, . . . will guide you into all truth; for He will not speak on His own authority, but whatever He hears He will speak; and He will tell you things to come" (John 16:13 NKJV).

Write down your answers to the questions and assignments. An old Chinese proverb says, "He who writes, tastes life twice." As you work through the questions and interac-tive portions, use the blanks to write your perspective and ideas. More than men-tally answering these questions, the writing process will allow for deeper life reflection and will concretely show you areas for needed growth. It will also high-light areas where you've already grown as a disciple of Christ. Your written pages give a lasting record of your commitments and discoveries that you can return to for a benchmark of your progress.

Select a leader (in a group context). It's rare that the dynamics of a group work properly unless someone is appointed the leader. Select a follower of Christ with leadership and discernment skills. The leader is a facilitator, one who will guide the discussion, make sure the group stays on relevant subjects, and provide everyone an opportunity to participate.

Encourage accountability. Whether you work through this in a group (one-on-one with another member) or as an individual, make a point to have one person as an accountability partner. This person will help "hold your feet to the fire" of accountability as you are rekindled. Seek to find a person who will allow you to be honest yet not judgmental—and who will keep a confidence. Despite high expectations and goals for ourselves, each of us falls short. But, if someone else holds us accountable when we fall off the horse, with His help and our accountability partner's, we can get back on again. Give this person permission to ask questions about your personal growth and to challenge you. Often such a relationship is the difference between simply reading the material and applying it to your daily life.

Whether you are seeking to draw closer to God in a group setting or alone, you'll find a couple of useful tools in the workbook that should help. There are readings and responses to complete each day, five days a week. Each day you will find what I call a "word bite." In a world of "sound bites," I've tried to give you a few "word bites" that make you think, worship, or even sing. These words are quotations, definitions, or, in some cases, lyrics to songs. Worship is key to rekindling our fire. Take time to read the word bites. Eat them. Offer them back to God. Write them down and post them in your world if they're particularly inspiring. Stop and sing the songs.

I have also included a key verse for each day. If you are in a group, members may want to recite these verses as part of the weekly meeting. I also recommend you choose one verse per week to memorize. (If you're meeting with a group, take time in the beginning to recite the verse to the group.) Hiding God's Word in our hearts and minds is vital to rekindling our spiritual fire.

In *Ignite Your Passion for God*, you can find anew your personal and loving God.

A word of warning, though. If your focus is on things confined to this earthly world, like getting ahead and acquiring more "stuff," this book will frustrate you; in fact, for you it's the wrong book! You will not find God in the things of this world. Instead, you and I will find Him through the pauses in the midst of our hurried lives, taking stock of who we are, and turning our faces toward Him. Our significance comes only from Christ. That's where revival begins.

God is calling the world to revival one heart at a time. Let's turn the page and get started.

1 A LIFE READY FOR REVIVAL

A revival is often thought of as a tent meeting during the summer, somewhere in the Bible belt. Shouting itinerant preachers predict doom for unrepentant sinners as they pound out their message on a wooden podium. "Bringing in the Sheaves" or "Amazing Grace" ring through the tent as the altar call is given.

"Come now and give your life to Jesus," the preacher says. "Recommit your life to Christ."

"Quit sinning. Quit drinking. Quit having sex outside marriage. You can't quit by yourself, but God can deliver you," the messenger explains. "Return to Him. Let God help you." Then he adds, "Don't let God pass you by!"

It sounds cliché, but many have come to salvation through these meetings. Commitments were real. God was present. But what happened when the meeting was over, when the preacher left, when the people resumed their daily lives?

For some, their relationship with God culminated at the end of the Sunday night meeting. For others, it was just a beginning. God met them in that tent, and nothing was ever the same. What made the difference? For the first group, "The Revival" was an event to be planned for, to be experienced, to come to an end. For the others, "revival" became a way of life. It wasn't a one-night or one-week experience, but rather how each day was begun, ended, and lived in between. A constant spiritual renewal of their relationship with Christ.

And that is true revival—an ongoing renewal within. Revival can never be reduced to a specific planned event. But revival does change lives, communities, and even the world.

DAY ONE

THE FOUNDATION–A
PERSONAL RELATIONSHIP

In Mississippi, as an eight year old in my church's biannual evangelistic event, called a "revival," I committed my life to Jesus Christ. It wasn't a hellfire-and-brimstone time. The pastor simply asked us, "Do you want to love God completely all your life?" He didn't storm his audience with sin, but talked about the love of Jesus. At the conclusion of his sermon, I responded to his invitation.

As I began to move forward, my neighbors in the pew tried to grab me. Luckily, I was so tiny—my nickname was Mouse—that they missed. They thought I was far too young to make such an important decision. Later the pastor agreed to talk with my parents, to pray about the validity of the decision. In the end, they all agreed, "This kid does know what he is doing."

Almost twenty years later, one of my cousins said to me, "You really met Jesus Christ that night when you were eight years old, didn't you?"

"Yes, I did," I said. "How could you tell?"

"Well, most of us in the South joined a church when we were young. And that's all we did. But you were different. Before that day, you were one of the meanest kids I had ever known, and you changed!"

> *The focus in revival is Jesus Christ, not revival. A genuine revival is characterized by a fresh revelation of the grace, greatness, and glory of Jesus Christ.*
>
> —◆—
>
> Mark Stibbe

I have many faults. If you want the details, talk with Ouida, my wife! The Christian life has been a continual growth experience for me, a pilgrimage. But by meeting Christ personally, my heart and life changed. I am still on that pilgrimage. These pages, I trust, will help you in your pilgrimage to grow in your relationship with Jesus Christ.

Take a moment and prayerfully respond to the questions and instructions that follow.

Have you met Jesus personally? Describe that experience.

_____

_____

The only way to understand the rest of this book is first to know Jesus Christ as Lord and Savior. The basis of our study in these pages is rooted in a relationship with Christ and His presence in our lives.

Turn in your Bible to Genesis 1:1, 27; John 1:3; and Romans 1:20. After reading these three verses, summarize God's presence in the world around you.

_____

_____

The Creator of the universe loves you and wants you to know Him intimately, presently, and forever. Consider what the Bible says about His love in 1 Timothy 2:1–4 and John 3:16. Look up these two passages, then write down your own paraphrase of what you learned about God's love. (Don't pass over John 3:16, an all-too-familiar verse for many.)

_____

_____

God has always loved you and will forever, whether you are His child or not. But we've been created with the free will to choose whether to receive that relationship. The first man and woman chose to disobey God and go their own willful way. Many still choose to disobey God, and it results in a broken relationship. God's heart breaks for these people.

See what the Bible says about this broken relationship in Romans 3:23 and Isaiah 59:2; then summarize what it says in your own words below.

_____

_____

Throughout history, an unholy people have tried to reach a holy God through various routes: religion, good works, ethics, morality, and philosophy—all without success. Our Father God has provided a way for us to have a restored relationship through Jesus Christ, and He is the only way. Because Jesus died on the cross for your sins, He took your punishment and made a way for the restoration of your relationship with God.

Examine these verses: 1 Timothy 2:5, Romans 5:8, and John 1:29, and summarize God's solution to a broken relationship.

_____

_____

God never forces us to respond. Each of us must accept that Jesus Christ paid for our sins through His death on the cross. As you give your life to Him, then you will have a right relationship with God.

Read Revelation 3:20, John 14:6, and John 1:12. What is your response to these verses?

_____

_____

If you have not given your life to Christ, is there any good reason why you shouldn't invite Him into your life right now? If you have already given your life to Christ, how is He calling you to greater depths?

Look up John 10:9. Summarize it below.

_____

_____

In the Bible, God gives each of us the vital steps to a personal relationship with Him:

1. Admit that you are a sinner (one who has rebelled against God; Romans 3:23).

2. Be willing to turn away from your sin and toward Christ (repent; Romans 4:7–8).

3. Believe that Christ died for your sins on the cross and rose from the dead, conquering sin and death for you (Romans 5:8).

4. Through prayer, invite Christ into your life as Lord and Savior. Commit your life to Him so He can take control through the Holy Spirit (Romans 10:9–10).

You can be assured of your salvation because of what God promises in His Word. What assurance do you receive from Romans 10:13 and Ephesians 2:8–9?

_____

_____

Whether you've just read these Bible verses for the first time or the thousandth time, they affirm a faith relationship with Jesus Christ that is immediate and eternal.

REVIEW THE DAY

Perhaps you have accepted Christ as a new believer. Or perhaps you have used this as an opportunity to renew your relationship. Use the space below to reflect on God's gift of new life.

What was the most meaningful sentence or Bible verse in this section? Rephrase that particular sentence or verse as a prayer to God.

_____

_____

_____

What action does God want you to take as a result of today's study? Meditate, think deeply, and listen to your heart; then write about the action you will take.

_____

_____

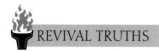

REVIVAL TRUTHS

- Revival is a lifetime process, not only a one-time event.
- A personal relationship with Jesus Christ is the beginning of revival.
- We can be assured of God's forgiveness through Scripture.

KEY VERSE

For whosoever shall call upon the name of the Lord shall be saved. (Romans 10:13)

DAY TWO

SPIRITUAL CALISTHENICS

After meeting Jesus personally, I began the discipline of reading the Bible and praying nearly every day. Even as a young boy, God showed me the need to be disciplined and purposeful in life. I had a clear set of personal guidelines. Each night before I went to bed, I read a chapter of Scripture. If I forgot, then the next morning I would read two. If something prevented my reading and I missed again, the next night I read three. With this primitive schedule, the chapters could stack up quickly. Fortunately, I was lazy enough to not want to get too far behind. It wasn't the purest motive, but it kept me on schedule. Through the discipline of Bible reading I was learning more about God. In the process, I was being changed, for something supernatural occurs in the heart when it absorbs the truth of God's Word.

In addition to reading Scripture, I began talking daily with God through prayer. That beginning of my relationship with God was the sweetest part of my childhood. I couldn't understand why anyone would not want to know God. If God made us and had a plan for our lives, then a person would be foolish not to know Him. Perhaps this view was a tangible example of coming to God as a child—living obediently through childlike faith. I was taught that reading Scripture and praying were the way to grow in my relationship with Christ, so I innocently obeyed.

When I was in high school our church had "cold turkey" visitation on Thursday evenings, where we knocked on doors in our neighborhood to talk with others about Christ. That may sound like bold intrusion today, but in the South in those days it was not. Back then, you usually didn't call ahead, you just stopped by. If it was at mealtime, you had a meal. If they were out on the tractor, you got on and rode along. The farmer kept working while he talked with you.

What an adventure! As a young boy, I went from a rewarding personal relationship to moving outside myself to share Christ with others. It was a logical progression of spiritual growth. I had been changed by God's love and wanted others to have the same opportunity. At times my testimony was openly received. At other times, it was not. What a shock to learn that not everyone had the contentment and security of a relationship with Jesus. What an even bigger shock to realize that many people rejected Christ.

Yet, it was these adventures of sharing my faith, along with prayer and Scripture study, that caused me to grow.

Think about your own life. Do you have a routine for prayer and Scripture study? Describe how you currently spend time with God.

_____

_____

Consider Philippians 4: 6–7. How does prayer affect our lives?

_____

_____

When was the last time you shared your faith with anyone out of obedience to God? Describe the experience.

_____

_____

Are you afraid to share your faith? Stop now and ask God to show you the root of this fear. What does He say to you?

_____

_____

It is not just prayer and sharing that help us to grow in our faith. God gives us many exercises to "flex" our spiritual muscles. Richard J. Foster, in his excellent book *Celebration of Discipline*, listed several disciplines for spiritual growth. He discussed corporate disciplines like worship that reflect our part in the body of Christ, our need to be connected with others. These outward disciplines, such as service, relate to the way we live. Foster also discussed inward disciplines, which include meditation, prayer, fasting, and study. While discipline is often seen as punishment, or at best a negative influence, Foster stated that "God has given us the Disciplines of the spiritual life as a means of receiving His grace. The Disciplines allow us to place ourselves before God so that He can transform us."[1]

> *Take my life, and let it be,*
> *Consecrated, Lord, to thee.*
>
> ———◆———
>
> "TAKE MY LIFE, AND LET IT BE"/Frances R. Havergal

In one of his sermons, my pastor, Jim Tomberline, also discussed spiritual disciplines. He referred to them as "habits of the heart." (Read 1 Timothy 4:7b–8.) What are the spiritual exercises that keep a person spiritually fit? Here are eight key areas that Pastor Tomberline noted:

1. Renew your strength through worship (Isaiah 40:31).
2. Deepen your peace of mind through prayer (Philippians 4:6–7).
3. Strengthen your commitment through fellowship (Hebrews 10:24–25).
4. Expand your perspective through biblical exposure (John 8:31–32).
5. Increase your joy through witnessing (1 Peter 3:15).
6. Practice your love through giving (2 Corinthians 8:7–8).
7. Develop your talents through serving (1 Peter 4:10).
8. Restore your soul through retreating (Matthew 11:28–29).[2]

Growing in our relationship with Christ requires discipline. The word *training* in 1 Timothy 4:7–8 comes from the Greek word *gumnazo*, from which we get *gymnasium*. It is continual discipline in training that produces growth. In athletics, one often hears, "No pain, no gain." It's a comfort to know that any pain we might encounter is merely a growing pain. With Jesus, who has gone before us, we are to "lay aside every weight, and the sin which doth so easily beset us, and . . . run with patience the race that is set before us" (Hebrews 12:1b).

REVIEW THE DAY

What strengths do you have in the area of spiritual discipline? Describe them.

_____

_____

In what areas do you need to grow? Describe those.

_____

_____

Ask God now to reveal to you His plan for your spiritual growth. Record that plan here.

_____

_____

What was the most meaningful sentence or Bible verse in this section? Rephrase that particular sentence or verse as a prayer to God.

_____

_____

_____

What action does God want you to take as a result of today's study? Meditate, think deeply, and listen to your heart; then write about the action you will take.

_____

_____

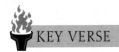

REVIVAL TRUTHS

- It is through spiritual discipline that we exercise our spiritual muscles for growth.
- Discipline is not punishment, but a way to put us before God so He can change our lives.

KEY VERSE

Let us lay aside every weight, and the sin which doth so easily beset us, and let us run with patience the race that is set before us. (Hebrews 12:1b)

DAY THREE

A GOD-DIRECTED LIFE

When I entered college, it was time to decide on a career. Medicine was a natural for me. I enjoyed people, I could think fast in an emergency, and I loved to witness while helping others. Medicine would be a great platform for sharing my faith because a doctor is often helping people in crisis as they consider serious life issues. But I felt a spiritual force pulling me toward the ministry, a pull I worked hard to ignore.

Around this time, my girlfriend, Ouida (who eventually became my wife), and I had been dating for two years. We came to a point in our relationship that we either needed to get married or break up. So we broke up—for two weeks!

During that time, I asked out another girl. We went to dinner and then returned to her apartment. While in the living room, I saw other couples, partially dressed, go in and out of a bedroom. I could see what was going on and walked out the apartment, probably hurting the girl's feelings. I didn't belong in the midst of such obvious temptation. I knew God watched over me all the time, but I was also young with budding hormones. The Bible said, "Flee youthful lusts"—so I did.

My date stood at the window watching me walk down the outside stairs of her apartment building. At the bottom step, I heard wise words speak to my mind: "What's more important? Helping someone live seventy years with quality of life, or helping someone live eternally?" God was speaking to me, and in an instant His profound, simple truth overwhelmed me. My legs lost all energy, and I fell to my knees. It was a *chairos* moment with God. I looked up to realize this girl was still watching me from her window above, while my weakened knees were glued to the concrete walkway. I couldn't get up.

I prayed, "God, you've got to let me get up. This is one of the most embarrassing experiences of my life." Finally I was able to get up and walk away, and probably to her delight, I never saw that girl again.

You'd think that after hearing God loud and clear I would have submitted to His call, but I still held on to my dream to become a doctor. Later that same summer, the Lord spoke to my mind again. "Tom, you're going to be a preacher." Immediately I protested. These were not the words I wanted to hear, even though I had been asking His direction for my life. Intellectually I wanted God's direction to be the same as my desire.

> *If we really knew just how much He loves us,*
> *we would always be willing*
> *to receive anything from His hand.*
>
> Brother Lawrence

One day during the early part of the summer, I read Billy Graham's syndicated column, "My Answer," in the *Daily Corinthian*, the local newspaper of Corinth, Mississippi. Dr. Graham wrote that he prayed about everything. He even prayed when he parked his car because if he prayed about where to park, then he could help people —as God guided him.

So I too began praying about where to park. Every time I prayed about parking I sensed God's direction, and each time I left my car someone with a need would be there. After helping them, I often had an opportunity to talk about Christ. It was amazing, and the many opportunities began to convict my heart because I thought, "Wow, God cares about all the details in people's lives, including mine. Even parking is important to Him. Well, if where to park is important, then everything is important—especially my calling in life."

Can God constantly direct your daily life? Write down a specific incident of the Lord's direction.

_____

_____

Perhaps you read this and feel discouraged, as though you may have missed God's call for your life. Remember that there is nothing wasted in the kingdom of God. Though my journey of faith started at a young age, God will begin with you

28

right now where you are, regardless of your stage in life. Don't be discouraged if you are farther along in life but just now beginning to follow His plan for you. Read Joel 2:25–26. How do these verses apply specifically to your life? As you can see, God will redeem lost years for His children.

As we grow in our relationship, we grow in our obedience, and His plan and purpose for our lives come forward. Perhaps you are not called into "professional" ministry, but you are called to minister as He directs in your daily life.

A complete study of God's will in your life is beyond the emphasis of this workbook, but let's take a few minutes to examine the life of Jesus. When Jesus Christ walked the earth, He carefully followed God's direction in His life. One of His keys to following God's will each day was to focus on God's desires and not His own. Read John 5:17–20.

Is God always working in today's world? In your life? What insight can you gain from John 5:17?

_____

_____

If we have a personal relationship with God, how can we live in accordance with God's will as seen in John 5:19?

_____

_____

What affirmation about living in God's will is found in John 5:20?

_____

_____

REVIEW THE DAY

It may be completely new to you to realize that God cares about the intimate details of your everyday life. Even if thinking about God's direction isn't new, it may be a good reminder for you. Use the space below to reflect on God's guidance in your own life.

_____

_____

God's direction in your life isn't always specific. The Lord wants you to trust Him step by step for His direction. Look at the lives of Peter, Andrew, James, and John. Notice how they obediently followed Jesus without reservation in Matthew 4:18–22.

How quickly do you respond to God's call? Explain your answer.

_____

_____

What was the most meaningful sentence or Bible verse in this section? Rephrase that particular sentence or verse as a prayer to God.

_____

_____

_____

What action does God want you to take as a result of today's study? Meditate, think deeply, and listen to your heart; then write about the action you will take.

_____

_____

REVIVAL TRUTHS

- Everything in your life is important to God.
- God will guide you in making decisions if you ask Him.

KEY VERSE

Then answered Jesus and said unto them, Verily, verily, I say unto you, the Son can do nothing of himself, but what he seeth the Father do: for what things soever he doeth, these also doeth the Son likewise. (John 5:19)

DAY FOUR

DECISION
TIME

As Billy Graham pointed out, God cares about our prayers for parking—and a lot more. After realizing God cares not just about parking, but about what I did with my life, I finally asked, "God, what do you want me to do?"

During the final night of another evangelistic campaign in my hometown, the voice that responded to my question was so booming I thought everyone in the church heard it—yet no one seemed to notice a thing. God was again speaking to my mind. I clung to the back of the pew with white knuckles, weeping because I realized God had called me to preach. It wasn't what I wanted. At the age of nineteen, my only goal was to be a wealthy physician. I didn't want to put up with church boards or elders or people who think they are the majority stockholders in the pastor's life. Raised in the church, I had seen preachers tormented by carnal congregation members. I didn't want that for me or my future family.

My mind was filled with stereotypes about pastors. I didn't want to eat a lot of chicken. I didn't want to get fat. I didn't want to spend days counting nickel-and-dime offerings. I didn't want to be a preacher, but I knew God had called me; I knew His voice. I wanted to trust Him, but I wept thinking of giving up *my* dreams to follow God's call.

From listening to God, I knew I should respond publicly and make a commitment, but I just didn't want to. I was proud and fearful. I didn't go forward. After the service that night, I was desperate to find Leroy Tubbs, our pastor. I felt like I would burst open. I finally spotted him outside the church. I grabbed him, jerked him into a side room off the narthex, and fell on his shoulder broken and bawling.

> *Shout to the Lord*
> *All the earth let us sing . . .*
> *Forever I'll love You,*
> *Forever I'll stand.*
> *Nothing compares to the promise I have in You.*
>
> ——◆——
>
> "SHOUT TO THE LORD"/Darlene Zschech

At first he didn't understand my tears, but when I finally could tell him, he rejoiced. Pastor Tubbs knew that God had been working in my heart for about two years, but neither of us could understand the purpose. At that moment, he knew. He encouraged me to transfer to a Bible college instead of returning to the University of Mississippi. After my decision to change careers, my concerned parents brought me back home to attend a local junior college. They thought I was mentally cracking up. As a pre-med student at Ole Miss, I was a success, making excellent grades, and they couldn't comprehend the apparently sudden switch in career choices.

Confusion reigned. I headed toward the pastorate, for I wanted to be obedient to God's call on my life. Meanwhile, my family and friends thought I was nuts and told me so. But I knew that God would guide my decisions. He had prompted me and was leading me. It was a *chairos* moment—a "Wow!" when God intervened in my life, and I responded.

God speaks in many ways but mostly through His Word. Can you pinpoint a time of your life when God's Word has spoken to you?

Through a "multitude of counsellors there is safety," the Bible says in Proverbs 11:14. How has God directed your life through other people? In a few words recall one of those incidents.

At times God also speaks in the still, small voice. Has a God-directed thought, prompting, or leading come into your mind during prayer or at another time? Summarize this occasion.

_____

_____

The Lord also speaks through circumstances of life—positively and negatively. How has God caught your attention through events and circumstances in your life? Note one below.

_____

_____

A key to any personal relationship is trust. Merriam-Webster's Collegiate Dictionary defines trust as "assured reliance on the character, ability, strength, or truth of someone or something." Have there been points in your life where you had to choose to trust God? Write a few words to remind yourself of one incident.

_____

_____

Are you at a point in your life now where you can trust God more deeply? Read Proverbs 3:5–6. How will this deeper trust guide you as you interact or impact the world around you?

_____

_____

REVIEW THE DAY

In your life, you have probably arrived at many forks in the road. List one of those decisions below and whether it was God-directed or human-directed.

_____

_____

Today make a fresh commitment to ask God to direct your life. Write a prayer with that commitment.

_____

_____

What was the most meaningful sentence or Bible verse in this section? Rephrase that particular sentence or verse as a prayer to God.

_____

_____

_____

What action does God want you to take as a result of today's study? Meditate, think deeply, and listen to your heart; then write about the action you will take.

_____

_____

REVIVAL TRUTHS

- Following Christ and His goals for our life is a matter of obedience.
- God speaks through the Scriptures, to our minds during prayer, and through other people.

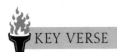

KEY VERSE

Trust in the Lord with all thine heart; and lean not unto thine own understanding. In all thy ways acknowledge him, and he shall direct thy paths. (Proverbs 3:5–6)

DAY FIVE

REVIVAL 101

Throughout this week, we have focused on our personal relationship with Christ. We've considered our initial commitment, the importance of spiritual disciplines, and the need to hear God and obey His call in our lives. These are the foundations for personal revival. Let's begin to look at revival as a concept that moves beyond our personal lives to impact the lives of others.

Lewis Drummond, a gifted evangelist and professor, became my mentor during seminary. Dr. Drummond loved to tell people how to know God, and I took every course I possibly could from him. One of those courses was entitled "Revival 101."

I went into the class with a preconceived notion of its content. To me, revival was an evangelistic campaign, and I thought this course would teach me the how-to's. I signed up believing I knew what to expect, but found something totally unexpected.

Dr. Drummond described great periods of history when the Holy Spirit moved on a people in a powerful fashion. He began in the Bible where God intervened in the affairs of men and women, then in history with nations transformed through His intervention, or *chairos* moments. Dr. Drummond challenged us regarding how such movements came through prayer, brokenness, and humility. Once an individual is spiritually broken, then God can intervene in a mighty manner.

I learned that revival is a continual process of brokenness and restoration, not just a one-night event or even a series of meetings. As I listened to his explanation, my heart jumped. I suddenly knew that I was born for revival and to be part of a spiritual awakening—an awakening that I believe is now in the embryonic stages of touching America and the world!

> ## Revival is . . .
> *Revival is about God. His children meeting*
> *with God, the nation being confronted with Him.*
>
> ———◆———
>
> Colin Urquhart

There are many glimmers of hope regarding this spiritual awakening, but here are a couple of examples. On October 4, 1997, an estimated one million men from all races and denominational backgrounds gathered in Washington, D.C., for prayer and reconciliation in an event organized by Promise Keepers, a group focused on bringing revival to the hearts of men. The event, "Stand in the Gap: A Sacred Assembly of Men," was reported to have been the largest religious gathering in American history. Spiritual and racial reconciliation has been enhanced immeasurably in recent years, and we have seen much greater trust and desire to work together locally and nationally from spiritual brothers and sisters of all ethnic groups and denominational backgrounds. It was only one instance of what God has been doing in hearts around the world.

Or consider that on September 17, 1999, approximately 3 million teenagers gathered at the flagpoles of their public schools to pray for their teachers, principals, parents, city leaders, and each other—unprecedented in the youth movements of history. The prayer time was heightened that year when the shootings and deaths of fourteen students and a teacher at Columbine High School in Littleton, Colorado, brought national attention to the teenage students who faced death because of their faith. And yet, out of the darkness of death in Littleton came beacons of light from students standing publicly, perhaps as never before, proudly proclaiming their faith. Church congregations grew; some reported doubling.[3] Revival came.

These signs of rekindled spiritual renewal are appearing across our world and nation. Each sign gives us hope and encouragement for our daily walk with Jesus Christ. As each person walks in obedience, God is able to weave those individual acts of obedience together into a greater move of His Spirit.

Being a goal-minded person, I determined a mission statement for my life. "I exist to help others know God personally through Jesus Christ through the spiritual awakening of the church and the resulting action which brings salvation to all possible and justice for all possible globally."

This seemed to be an impossible mission statement to fulfill. Alan Redpath, a great British preacher, told me in 1983 that when God wants to do an impossible thing, He takes an impossible man (or woman) and crushes him. God uses the broken vessel He reconstructs. Be encouraged.

God's ways are a part of my daily life as I die to Tom and open myself by faith to Him. As I experience personal revival, and grow in my intimacy with Christ, it increases my desire to be obedient to His Word and also to share Him with others. And as others experience personal revival, they will live more holy lives and share Christ too. Again, be encouraged.

We desire to see the reality of 2 Chronicles 7:14. Read that verse now. We pray for a spiritual awakening in the United States. We want God to heal our land. For God to heal the land, He must heal one person at a time, beginning with you and me.

In a world full of self-help and New Age teaching, how is our hope for revival found in Christ alone? Look at Paul's warning to the church in Colosse encouraging us to turn to Jesus (Colossians 2:8–9).

_____

_____

If revival is to spread, it must begin with individuals. How is this described in Matthew 5:13–16?

_____

_____

REVIEW THE DAY

More than any other time in recent history, Americans are aware of their growing spiritual needs. Printed material on spirituality has been in great demand during recent years. Why? It's an indicator of the searching heart.

Define revival for your personal life.

_____

_____

What was the most meaningful sentence or Bible verse in this section and why? Rephrase that particular sentence or verse as a prayer to God.

_____

_____

_____

What action does God want you to take as a result of today's study? Meditate deeply, and listen to your heart; then write about the action you will take.

_____

_____

 REVIVAL TRUTHS

- World revival begins with personal revival, through *chairos* moments with God.
- Personal revival begins with daily and consistent intimacy with God through prayer and Bible study.
- Personal revival requires daily obedience to His call.

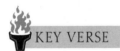 KEY VERSE

Ye are the light of the world. A city that is set on an hill cannot be hid . . . (Matthew 5:14)

LOOKING AHEAD

Revival begins in the hearts of individuals. As we personally experience revival, growing out of a relationship with Christ, we then share this hope with others. It's a process that bears the fruit of God in our lives—not an event. Next week we will learn about the methods God uses to bring us to a point of personal revival.

2 SPIRITUAL BROKENNESS

The journey to rekindle the fire of your passion for Christ often begins at an unlikely spot. It begins with a word not usually spoken from the pulpit today, yet it was fully recognized by the early church fathers as the route for spiritual wholeness: *brokenness.*

Our world displays plenty of examples opposing brokenness—examples of pride. Pride is the slogan of the day on Madison Avenue. "You deserve it. You can make it yourself. You are capable and independent and sufficient." The big You—without need of God. Pride puffs you up rather than allowing you to realize your own inadequacies, your humanness, your dependence on Him. Ironically that's what sets you free.

During this week, let's examine the concept of spiritual brokenness. What does it mean? How do you discover it? What impact can it have to rekindle your love relationship with Jesus Christ?

DAY ONE

PITIFUL PRIDE

God can't use a prideful person. The Bible says, "Pride goeth before destruction, and an haughty spirit before a fall" (Proverbs 16:18). Paraphrasing St. Augustine, pride in who you truly are in Christ is not a sin, but pride in who you think you are, inordinate pride, is a sin. It's perfectly normal to be glad that you are a child of God or a joint heir with Christ, but we're talking here about pride in yourself apart from God.

In my own journey with pride and brokenness, I have gone through several stages, and I expect more stages will come. The first stage I experienced was an awareness of pride in my life. As with most issues, God worked through circumstances and other people to bring this to light.

During high school, I competed in the high hurdles track-and-field event. During the regionals, I had one last chance to go to the state championship, and I felt confident I would qualify. The runners lined up, the gun sounded, but there was a false start—someone left the starting blocks too soon. We returned to our positions. The second time the gun sounded, I saw another false start. There was a difference this time, however. I saw it, but the official did not. He didn't signal it false. Confident I was right, however, I had halted in the blocks until I saw the entire field race ahead of me. I finally took off, chasing the pack.

As I started clearing those hurdles, I *knew* the guys around me started early. I was sure the official would call us back to the starting line. Yet the race continued, and no false start was called. I had to push hard to catch them. To qualify for state, you had to finish either first or second in the heat. I came in third. Afterward my coach asked, "Why did you stop?"

"Coach, it was a false start."

He said, "Yeah, but you aren't the one who calls it false, are you?" I was devastated. I knew I was good enough to compete at the state level, but my pride kept me from achieving my goal. Right wasn't right that time.

> ## *Revival is . . .*
> *that strange and sovereign mark of God in which*
> *He visits His own people, restoring, reanimating,*
> *and releasing them into the fullness of His blessing.*
>
> Stephen Olford

Looking back, I am grateful now to see God's hand in these situations. I had an enormous amount of pride, and I argued a lot, convinced I was always right. I don't remember ever losing a debate or argument throughout high school or college or even during points in my marriage, but I believe I lost friends and at times alienated my wife. God needed to deal with my pride. He continues to deal with my pride. It requires daily confession and repentance. My desire is that I would be humble before God, but sometimes I still struggle. I want to be worthy of use by God, but His vessel needs periodic purifying.

Do you understand the meaning of inordinate, or inappropriate pride? Do you have inordinate pride in your life? Write down what it means to you and a word about whether you have it or not.

_____

_____

On a scale between 1 and 10 (1=low and 10=very high) evaluate the level of your own inordinate pride, and why you think you're giving a fair rating.

_____

_____

What does God think about pride? For some insight, see Job 20:6–7, Psalm 101:5, Proverbs 16:5, and Isaiah 23:9.

_____

_____

Read Genesis 3:1–3. The temptation to sin wasn't related to eating a particular piece of fruit. Satan enticed Eve by speaking to her pride. He said:

"You won't die. Even though God said you would, it won't happen to you."

"You deserve to be as smart as God—don't you?"

"C'mon, you deserve it."

What are some of the results of pride? Examine Job 35:12, Proverbs 13:10, and Proverbs 29:23 before you answer.

_____

_____

Consider how pride affected King Nebuchadnezzar in Daniel chapters 4 and 5. What were the consequences for the king?

_____

_____

REVIEW THE DAY

God hates the proud and eventually allows them to be humbled. There are always consequences to pride in our lives.

What have been some of the consequences of pride in your life?

_____

_____

43

Review Psalm 51:17. Today make a fresh commitment to remove inordinate pride in your life. Write a prayer with that commitment below.

_____

_____

What was the most meaningful sentence or Bible verse in this section? Rephrase that particular sentence or verse as a prayer to God.

_____

_____

_____

What action does God want you to take as a result of today's study? Meditate, think deeply, and listen to your heart; then write about the action you will take.

_____

_____

 REVIVAL TRUTHS

- Whether or not you are aware of it, pride can hinder your relationship with the eternal God.
- The Lord wants you to consider pride in your life, then remove it. He wants you to be proud only of Him, and His work in and through your life.

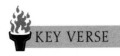 KEY VERSE

A man's pride shall bring him low: but honour shall uphold the humble in spirit. (Proverbs 29:23)

DAY TWO

RUSTY PIPES

Recently I met with an ex-professional football player, now in the NFL Hall of Fame and in his early eighties. He's a truly great man and a dear friend. In spite of his age, God is still working on this physical and spiritual giant's pride. He was experiencing some personal difficulties, and he asked me, "Why is this happening in my life?"

"Is it possible God is working on your pride?" I asked.

Instantly he responded, "I don't have any pride."

"Oh really? Maybe that's the problem. When you think you don't have any pride, then that's when you may struggle with this very issue."

The giant of a man looked at me with a shocked expression. He said nothing—one of the few times I have known him to be at a loss for words.

Consider the promise of 2 Timothy 2:21: "If a man therefore purge himself from these [things not of God], he shall be a vessel unto honour, sanctified, and meet for the master's use, and prepared unto every good work."

Do you want to be prepared for every good work? Do you want God to use you as a holy vessel? If so, then you must get anything extraneous and unnecessary out of the way, often beginning with pride. The Bible tells us that personal character flaws are difficult to see, and pride is often the foundational flaw to keep us from seeing other issues. For that reason, God may use other people and circumstances to reveal our pride. The Bible says that "iron sharpens iron" (Proverbs 27:17 NKJV). We can sharpen one another's lives.

"Here is the outstanding feature of revival: Suddenly, without warning, God is present, and the people are brought face to face with God's holiness and their sin. It seems that God is dealing with them alone so that whatever the spiritual state of the person, saved or unsaved, a mighty work of transformation occurs. The unsaved are brought to salvation and the saved are brought to further holiness."

Dale Schlafer[1]

Recently, I saw a building containing a huge steam plant for a large complex. Projecting out of this building were several huge pipes. At key points the pipes were bent at right angles. An engineer, Madison Morris, explained to me the strange-looking pipes: "That's the steam plant, and the steam comes out in force. If we don't constrict the flow by making it go through several turns, it will blow the pressure valves when it hits the radiators in other buildings." The engineers reduced the power of the steam by hindering its flow.

Unlike the steam pipe, where too much power poses a danger, God wants us to have the unrestricted power of the Holy Spirit. Picture God's heart connected to your heart by a pipe. Is there rust in your pipe that keeps the power of the Holy Spirit from flowing freely into your thoughts and everyday actions? The rust may not block the pipe entirely, yet any time the flow of the Holy Spirit has to go around constrictions, it cuts down the power of the flow. Or do you have a lot of bending in your pipes, where you try to go around things God has for you? Our pipes should be straight, open to the flow of God's Holy Spirit.

We humans try to "clean" our spiritual pipes by self-revelation, self-actualization, and self-renewal. These self-centered activities will prove useless and frustrating. Conviction, confession, and turning to Him for cleansing are the keys to an unhindered flow of the Holy Spirit. Only God can remove the rust and straighten the pipes.

We need personal brokenness and humility, and then God can heal our land. God heals the land as He flows through unconstricted vessels, and you are one of those precious vessels. People mistakenly believe that worldwide revival happens when God opens the windows of heaven and pours the Holy Spirit from a big bucket.

That's not the way it works. The Holy Spirit flows through God's people, His vessels—one at a time.

So, if God is working in your heart, asking you to release your pride and submit to Him, then you, as an individual, are a key part of corporate revival. We are the means through which God reaches this world.

Consider your vessel. Is there rust in your pipes? Are they constricted? What rust needs to be removed? Pray now for God to clear the rust.

How can you strengthen yourself for God's service? Consider four key areas mentioned in Scripture: prayer, exercise and diet, telling others about God and His Son, and fasting. Read the following verses and make personal applications to your life.

Increased prayer: James 5:15–16

_____

_____

Exercise and diet: 1 Corinthians 6:19–20

_____

_____

Talking about God with others: Colossians 4:5–6

_____

_____

Fasting: Matthew 6:16, 18

_____

_____

REVIEW THE DAY

It's difficult to stand outside yourself and see character flaws. You need others to help you see areas for growth. It is through brokenness that we are able to grow, and as you continually grow in Christ, the power of the Holy Spirit can flow through your life.

Today, how are you working on the "rust" in your pipes so God's power can flow into and through your life? Write a prayer with your goal for the day below.

_____

_____

What was the most meaningful sentence or Bible verse in this section? Rephrase that particular sentence or verse as a prayer to God.

_____

_____

What action does God want you to take as a result of today's study? Meditate, think deeply, and listen to your heart; then write about the action you will take.

_____

_____

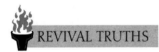

REVIVAL TRUTHS

- God uses brokenness to build strength into our lives.
- God desires to "clean our pipes."
- We need to be prepared for God to work through us.

KEY VERSE

If a man therefore purge himself from these, he shall be a vessel unto honour, sanctified, and meet for the master's use, and prepared unto every good work. (2 Timothy 2:21)

DAY THREE

BECOMING ACCOUNTABLE

Several years ago, one of my friends, Joe Leininger, moved from Chicago to Colorado Springs where we live. For ten years he had traded in the Eurodollar pit of the Chicago Mercantile Exchange, and his unusual business experiences are captured in a book, *Lessons from the Pit*.[2] Two weeks after he arrived, Joe and I met for lunch at a local deli. He said, "I have a request. Would you disciple me?"

My answer surprised Joe. "No, I don't do that." He looked at me oddly, certain I had discipled other men. After all, for over twenty years, I worked with Billy Graham and my spiritual mentor, Charlie Riggs, a discipler of men.

He said, "I thought you did that."

"No. You have to be consistently available to disciple someone, and I travel too much. But I will be in a Barnabas/John Mark relationship with you. I'm older so I'll be Barnabas and you be John Mark—brothers in Christ with a commitment to each other. The only commitment I will make is one you have to make to me too—I'll challenge you to grow as I see things in your life, but only if you'll help me grow. Like iron sharpening iron, the relationship has to be a two-way street. I need to learn too. I'm teachable and want to grow."

Joe accepted this condition, and we began to meet. After laying ground rules to discuss our growth in Christ, I dug into the conversation. "All right. The first thing I want to discuss is brokenness."

He said, "I don't want to talk about brokenness."

"Why not?"

"Because I don't like brokenness," Joe said, leaning on the table with sincerity. "It's like you're weak or something." His response wasn't surprising considering he had been a University of Illinois athlete and then spent years in the competitive locker room-like environment of the Chicago trading pit. In either of those situations, one would not wisely show weakness.

I responded, "No, it's not weakness at all. It is strength. There is strength in weakness. Paul says that the less you have the more you depend on Him. The Bible also says that when you are weak, He can be strong in you" (2 Corinthians 12:10).

Joe was adamant, saying again, "I don't want to talk about that."

"OK, we're not going to meet together then," I said, "because that's what God is doing in my life right now. He's continually breaking the old me, and I need it. Not that I like the pain of being broken, but I believe in the end result. If you are going to meet with me, then we'll talk about brokenness."

Reluctantly he said, "OK, if that's what it takes."

Again I affirmed, "That's the only way I can do it because it's where I am. I can't change from where I am in my growing relationship with Christ."

A few months later, Joe wrote in a letter, "You taught me a great deal about what it means to be a man of God. I no longer associate the idea of brokenheartedness with a killjoy Christian paranoia. Now I see it as the sort of humility that is needed for God to truly use a person to accomplish his purposes."

Revival is . . .
the going of God among His people.

━━━◆◆◆━━━

Duncan Campbell

Look at Proverbs 27:17. Who is the iron sharpener in your life?

_____

_____

We tend to place the apostles, such as Peter and Paul, on a pedestal as role models. Look at Paul's words about Peter in Galatians 2:8–14. Note how Paul confronted Peter. What was this situation and how was it resolved through accountability?

_____

_____

Do you have an accountability partner to help you with character issues such as pride? If not, find one, possibly with the help of your local church leader. Establish a few ground rules for your session together such as:

- The purpose of our meeting is to talk about areas of growth.
- Our conversation will be confidential.
- Our partnership is equally balanced—each person has an opportunity for growth.
- We'll commit to pray for each other.
- We'll commit to a regular schedule of meeting together.

As you evaluate a person as an accountability partner also consider: (1) Is this someone I enjoy meeting with on a regular basis? (2) Is this someone I can trust with my confidences? (3) Is this someone I can see meeting with over a long period of time? (4) Will this person's schedule or heart allow for a commitment to this relationship?

When you meet together, one way to promote deep conversation is with a series of questions. Each party should agree to these questions and their use ahead of time. John Maxwell, founder of The INJOY Group in Atlanta, suggests using questions to guide your meetings. Questions might include: (1) Are you reading your Bible and praying every day? (2) Consider what's running through your thoughts. Are they pure? (3) Are you misusing or violating any trust that someone else has given you? (4) Are you living every day in total obedience to God? Maxwell mentions that partial obedience equals disobedience.[3]

Then ask a fifth and final question: Have you lied about any of the previous questions? You may think the fifth question is unnecessary, but it's another call into accountability. Without penalty, it gives the person an opportunity to revisit any of the previous four questions.

REVIEW THE DAY

If you are serious about working on your pride and other character issues, you need accountability with someone else. My accountability relationship has fostered significant growth in my Christian life, and I'm convinced we can continue growing in our love relationship with Christ through accountability with another person.

Do you have such a person in your life? If so, write the name below. If not, then write a brief plan of how you will move toward such a relationship.

_____

_____

Read 1 John 1:9. Why is confession to others good for us? How does it apply in your life?

_____

_____

What was the most meaningful sentence or Bible verse in this section? Rephrase that particular sentence or verse as a prayer to God.

_____

_____

_____

What action does God want you to take as a result of today's study? Meditate, think deeply, and listen to your heart; then write about the action you will take.

_____

_____

REVIVAL TRUTHS

- Pride and other character issues are hard to see in ourselves.
- For character development, we need to have an accountability relationship.

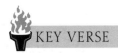

KEY VERSE

Iron sharpeneth iron; so a man sharpeneth the countenance of his friend. (Proverbs 27:17)

DAY FOUR

A NORMAL RELATIONSHIP WITH GOD

As you seek the heart of God in your pilgrimage, you will more readily accomplish God's purpose in your life. Some people think that brokenness is abnormal, but from the Bible, we learn that it's really the foundation on which God can build.

Our normal relationship with God hinges on the ability to communicate with Him on a consistent basis. The Bible says that we can "pray without ceasing" (1 Thessalonians 5:17). God has told us that we "ought always to pray" (Luke 18:1). This means that our hearts should be in utter communion with Him. Of course, it's so easy for us to move away from God and follow the ways of the world that seem to bring us possessions and power but often do not bring us joy. Even our thoughts are vitally involved in this process.

When I was dating Ouida, I met her Methodist minister, Jack Williams, a remarkable man. Reverend Williams led his church with tremendous spiritual depth and was one of the most godly men I'd ever met. As a high school student, when I went to church with her, I was always impressed by his emphasis on consistent prayer and our thought life. Every Sunday he opened the altar of his suburban Methodist church and people flooded to the front for communion with the Lord—individually and corporately. It was a sweet time. The power of the Holy Spirit was deeply present.

Each Sunday Brother Jack had a habit of handing out a little mimeographed piece of paper with a quotation on it, which always meant much to me as I meditated on each one. One touched my heart deeply, and I remember it to this day. It said, "What's in the conscious mind sinks down into the unconscious to influence our moods and our health. If we indulge negative, resentful, impure, or unkind thinking, we become tense and have a depressed spirit as individuals. But, if we fill our lives with what is positive, worthy and beautiful, we gradually grow poised, power-filled lives."

That quotation applies to Philippians 4:8–9. Read that now and paraphrase it below.

_____

_____

Our thoughts and actions are vitally connected in the normal Christian faith. They produce a flow in the relationship with God. In context this simply means "being occupied with God and seeing ourselves in relationship with Him. It means that we see ourselves as creatures but we see Him as Creator."[4]

What some people see as brokenness is alignment with His will and purpose for our lives. God wants to work His perfect will through us as He says in Philippians 2:13, "For it is God which worketh in you both to will and to do of His good pleasure." That is our normal Christian life—allowing God to flow through us unhindered.

> ### Revival is . . .
> *nothing more than a return to normal Christianity.*
>
> Tom Phillips

When I was a college senior, I needed a one-hour, upper-level art course to graduate. With only one summer left to complete a double major in biology and English, my opportunities to secure an art course were limited, and to my chagrin the only one that I could take was pottery. I couldn't believe that was a course they gave credit for in a university.

But, to my utter amazement, I loved the course and did well in it.

One day, at the wheel, as my feet moved rapidly on the stone below that turned the table above, I placed a ball of clay. Most pottery pieces begin with a thumb hole in the middle of the clay, and then with deft finger movements the clay is pulled into a tube and widened into the desired shape. That day I pulled the tallest and best tube I'd ever made. I was overjoyed. But to my horror I inadvertently stuck a hole in the side with my finger.

I looked at the clay on my finger and with relief realized that I could affix the lump back into the hole and smooth it out. Delighted, I began to push my feet against the wheel and bring the upper table to full momentum. I began to work the clay only to watch the reattached lump finally shoot off and fall to the floor. Oh, well, so much for repairing a broken vessel. I had to crush it and start over.

It is similar with our relationship to God. Though He does not make mistakes in fashioning us, He desires a perfect vessel. With each blemish, our loving Father uses brokenness to make us more like Him. It is not enough to be repaired, it requires a new start. It's normal life on the Potter's wheel.

The imagery of God the potter is told well by the prophet Jeremiah. Read Jeremiah 18:1–10; then summarize the verses.

_____

_____

How are we like the pot God described?

_____

_____

Are you willing to let God shape you into the pot of His choosing? Explain your answer.

_____

_____

REVIEW THE DAY

Initially we may resist the process of brokenness, but it's a normal act of faith in our pilgrimage with God. Read Isaiah 66:2. Evaluate your personal relationship with God. Are there any barriers in that relationship? If so, write them below.

_____

_____

Today make a fresh commitment to view your life as God sees you—flaws and all. How can you continue moving toward spiritual intimacy with Christ through brokenness?

_____

_____

Below write a prayer and ask God to touch your life in a fresh manner.

_____

_____

_____

What was the most meaningful sentence or Bible verse in this section? Rephrase that particular sentence or verse as a prayer to God.

_____

_____

_____

What action does God want you to take as a result of today's study? Meditate, think deeply, and listen to your heart; then write about the action you will take.

_____

_____

REVIVAL TRUTHS

- Constructive brokenness is a normal part of our life with Christ.
- Without brokenness, sin hardens our hearts to God's work in us.

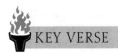

KEY VERSE

For all those things hath mine hand made, and all those things have been, saith the Lord: but to this man will I look, even to him that is poor and of a contrite spirit, and trembleth at my word. (Isaiah 66:2)

DAY FIVE

THE KEY TO NATIONAL HEALING: BROKENNESS

Only one thing prevents Jesus from filling our cup—sin. And the dirtiness in the cup of America looms large as we're absorbed with ourselves: our self-image, self-indulgence, self-pity, self-complacency, and self-seeking. The source of these "self-exhortations" is unbelief, an inverted form of pride. They hinder our intimacy with Christ.[5]

Such is our nation. In the article "Prodigal Nation," published by *Washington Watch*, Peter Marshall wrote that the United States has become a prodigal in the following ways. We have:

- rejected the "right way to do things" . . . in every . . . area of American life.
- trashed the reputations of our nation's founders.
- ended the practice of reforming our society in light of God's Word.
- rejected education with a Biblical worldview.
- rejected the notion of our founding fathers that "religion is the basis and foundation of government" (James Madison).
- rejected the fact that our constitution only works when the people whom it governs are moral and religious.
- rejected Benjamin Franklin's comment that "only virtuous people are capable of freedom."
- rejected the fact Americans of faith must be involved in current and moral civil government.[6]

This leaves us ripe for the judgment of God. The decadence of our society, the corruption of our religious leaders, and the ever-present example of abortion make us a prodigal nation.

We know God is concerned for our nation. In many ways the Lord holds the church of Jesus Christ responsible for the nation. Yes, the church is made up of people just like you and me. Therefore, as we look at the concerns relative to our nation, we as individuals must address the hope that is in Christ for the entire nation. Revival in the church is the way God will bring a renewal to our country. The foundation for that is brokenness and prayer. We all must pray, believing He has a plan for our nation and that the power of the Holy Spirit has defeated the enemy.

> ### *Revival is . . .*
> *God bending down to the dying embers of fire that is just about to go out, and breathing into it, until it bursts again into flame.*
>
> ———⊱⋅⊰———
>
> Christmas Evans

Matthew Henry once said, "When God intends great mercy for His people, He first of all sets them a-praying."[7] Through the efforts of the Mission America Coalition in 2000 and beyond, we *are* seeing a praying nation, with a goal of 3 million prayer "Lighthouses." A.T. Pierson said that "There has never been a spiritual awakening in any country or locality that did not begin in united prayer."[8]

Prayer and brokenness are united in the principles of 2 Chronicles 7:14. Read that verse and summarize it here.

_____

_____

As we are humble, convicted, and obedient, God can heal our land. What can we do to open the door for God to heal our land? We can:

- Die to self.
- Ask God to cleanse and purify our hearts.
- Ask God to search our hearts for bitterness or hate. Ask for forgiveness and make amends.
- Lift Christ's love above our differences so He is what others see in us. We can do this without changing our convictions.

- Be open to confession and repentance for historic acts relative to the way one people group has treated another, both in this nation and in the world.
- Condemn violence toward other people because of racial, ethnic, or any other types of difference.
- Realize that, though some sins are less "socially acceptable," we're all sinners in God's eyes.
- Love others who express differences in their lives, even if those differences are sinful. The saint must truly love the sinner regardless of the sin.

Brokenness in our nation will come when believers humble themselves before God. With that humility, God can pour His spirit into our lives, and through our lives into the lives of others.

Read Deuteronomy 8. The passage discusses God's past faithfulness to Israel and the country's dependence on God, but also the nation's subsequent waywardness. In what ways has the United States followed the example of ancient Israel?

_____

_____

What promises does God offer in verses 6–9, 18; to those who obey?

_____

_____

Reread verse 19–20. What will happen to those who do not obey?

_____

_____

REVIEW THE DAY

National brokenness is necessary for God to heal our land. What do you see from current events that reveals a national trend of pain and brokenness? Write it below.

_____

_____

People are apathetic about community involvement. Consider your own role. What action can you take in your community to make a difference? List one step that you commit to make in the next month.

_____

_____

What was the most meaningful sentence or Bible verse in this section? Rephrase that particular sentence or verse as a prayer to God.

_____

_____

_____

What action does God want you to take as a result of today's study? Meditate, think deeply, and listen to your heart; then write about the action you will take.

_____

_____

REVIVAL TRUTHS

- We can see the pillars of our nation crumbling; yet they crumble with God's purpose to return a nation with a broken, humble spirit to the Lord.
- National brokenness begins with personal brokenness.

KEY VERSE

But thou shalt remember the Lord thy God: for it is he that giveth thee power to get wealth, that he may establish his covenant which he sware unto thy fathers, as it is this day. (Deuteronomy 8:18)

LOOKING AHEAD

Brokenness is the antithesis of all that modern culture promotes. Pride is the foundation for many sinful behaviors. We think we're too good or too smart to let one little sin enslave us. Or we think we're more pure and holy than others who commit less "socially acceptable" sins. It's pride. In God's upside-down kingdom, it's the weak who are strong and the broken who are whole. Let's look ahead: Once we are open to brokenness, God can convict us and call us to freedom through *repentance*. That is the R word, the next step in revival.

3 THE R WORD

Spiritual revivals throughout history have another common thread—repentance. Many people are praying for God to touch the United States. Though the corporate need is certainly present, it will only begin as individuals turn from sin and turn to Christ.

When a military officer does an about-face, he turns from one direction and heads resolutely in the opposite. That's a picture of repentance. If, as a Christian, you have turned from God in any area of your life, ask God to convict you of your sin, and to help you see it as He does. Then as you confess this sin, agree with Him that it's wrong. Next, turn from repeating the sin as you turn toward God.

We often don't realize what it means to be a "normal" follower of Christ. Words like *confession* or *repentance* are whispered or never spoken. But confession and repentance are normal Christian experiences in our daily walk with Christ. They are good actions that help us overcome evil.

DAY ONE

REVIVAL REQUIRES REPENTANCE

Today's world has an urgency and desperation unlike any other period of history. The darkness in the world seems cavernous, and only a few pinpoints of light are breaking through. But those laser points from God do shine. We must remember that darkness never defeats light. Repentance opens the door for God's light to shine through.

Most people stop at confession and don't enter the next step, repentance. Some don't like the word *repentance* because it is connected with sin, and we don't like the word *sin*. Sin is putting the "I" before God. Conviction says, "Yes, God, I put myself before you." Confession says, "I will get the *I* out of the way in these specific areas." Most people think of confession as a horrendous guilt trip. Confession isn't negative; it's God's design to allow us to come to Him for cleansing.

Be man or woman enough to confess your sins or failures to God. He already knows. Confession comes from two words that mean to simply agree with God. Say something like, "God, I agree with you that I was unduly angry in that situation." Or "God, I agree that pride clouded my judgment in that situation." Confession, or agreeing that you have sinned, must always precede repentance, which is turning from that sin.

Read Leviticus 26:40–45. What are the benefits of confession to God?

Finally, there is repentance: turning from sin to Jesus Christ. It is not a crushing blow from God, but surrender into His loving arms. Imagine your life like that of a wise pilot. If he continued heading toward the mountain, he would crash; continue heading into sin, and you may crash into the mountain of spiritual separation from God, ruining your life. Instead, the pilot—and the believer—turn away from the mountain (sin and death) and heads for the airport of Jesus Christ. That's repentance.

A person who is reveling in his or her humanness and personal accomplishments doesn't want to be convicted or broken, doesn't want to confess and repent. That person's spiritual temperature is low; fears bend the individual. He doesn't desire the quiet place of introspection. The flesh is a constant battleground, which is why Paul said that he warred against his flesh.

I can tell when I am "in the flesh." If Ouida and I disagree on something, I will win if I'm not careful—right from my flesh. I know it's not God's Spirit in me, so I have to back off. I've made a commitment to my wife that I would not go for the jugular in an argument—that's the old Tom. I have repented of that sin and desire to turn from it.

I talked over this particular struggle with Joe Leininger, my accountability partner, and he said, "Tom, you've probably won so much in your life that now Ouida needs to win nine to one just to catch up for the past." Of course, Joe is right.

Even when we see our faults, a voice inside says, "Don't apologize." Or it says, "Deal with it later." Unfortunately those comments leave us in denial and "later" never comes. If you want to deepen your relationship with Jesus Christ, then immediately apologize to Him for rebelling—despite the embarrassment. Then confess and repent—first to God, and then to any person you have hurt by your sin.

When our daughter Molly was about twelve years old, I began to understand and be sensitive to the many flaws in my life. They were habitual flaws like impulsiveness or intensity or lack of patience—qualities that can put great burdens on other people living or working with me. And those flaws can lead to sin. I also struggled with my speech. Through my sharp tongue, I periodically put Molly and other members of our family on the spot.

Look, I determined, *I'm just going to begin confessing my sin immediately, apologize, and deal with this habitual problem. I am not going to let it ride and ignore it.* My flaws surfaced so often that I feared my apologies would become meaningless to my children and my wife, though I was sure God would understand, accept, and appreciate my repentance. I sat with my family and declared the five areas that I felt God wanted to change in my life. I told them, "I will ask for your forgiveness immediately and I am sincere about it—even though I may do it many times."

Months later, my wife told me that Molly declared, "I'm just sick of this."

"What are you sick about?" Ouida inquired.

Molly is a child similar to her dad and impulsively said, "I'm sick of Dad saying that he's sorry all of the time."

My wife told me that Molly thought for a minute, and then declared, "But, I'm so glad he does." My daughter knew the difference between a dad who infrequently declared his sorrow, who didn't repent, compared to my numerous apologies and continuing commitment to change.

> *Change my heart, oh God,*
> *make it ever true.*
> *Change my heart, oh God,*
> *May I be like You.*
>
> ———
>
> "CHANGE MY HEART OH GOD"/Eddie Espinosa

Read the following verses. Write a personal application for your own life after each one.

Acts 3:19

_____

_____

Revelation 2:4–5

_____

_____

Jeremiah 15:19

_____

_____

 REVIEW THE DAY

Have you considered repentance as a step beyond confession? How can repentance bring spiritual revival?

_____

_____

Take a moment now and pray. Ask God to show you areas where you have confessed sin, but not sought to truly repent. Record what God is saying to you.

_____

_____

What was the most meaningful sentence or Bible verse in this section? Rephrase that particular sentence or verse as a prayer to God.

_____

_____

_____

What action does God want you to take as a result of today's study? Meditate, think deeply, and listen to your heart; then write about the action you will take.

_____

_____

REVIVAL TRUTHS

- Repentance is moving beyond confessing sin to turning away from sin.
- Revival, either personal or corporate, cannot occur without repentance.

KEY VERSE

Therefore thus saith the Lord, If thou return, then will I bring thee again, and thou shalt stand before me: and if thou take forth the precious from the vile, thou shalt be as my mouth: let them return unto thee; but return not thou unto them. (Jeremiah 15:19)

DAY TWO

CONTROL
AND CONVICTION

Confession and repentance are not possible without conviction. It requires boldness to pray for conviction and a heart softened to hear God's voice directly through prayer, Scripture, or other people. Many people avoid situations where they might feel convicted. It's not a fun feeling.

Conviction also requires that we give up control, which is something our American culture teaches us never to do. We must release control from thinking that we know ourselves best. We must release control from thinking that we are always right. We must give up control from thinking that we can always act and respond exactly as we choose. We must release control from believing that we are a finished product, rather than a work in process. As long as we hold tightly to the reins of control, conviction will not come.

God brings conviction down many avenues. It is better to seek conviction than hide from it. By actively seeking those areas where God wants to change you, you will be more able to cooperate with the Holy Spirit as He works, which is always a better way.

You can seek conviction through prayer. Ask God to reveal to you areas of your life, your character, your personality, or your emotions that He would like to change. Wait on Him; He will answer. Another way is to look in the mirror of Jesus Christ and study Him. Study a Gospel like Mark and ask God to clearly reveal Jesus to you. Then ask Him to show you yourself in light of Himself.

God loves you and knows you desire to grow in your relationship with Him. Stop now and ask God to show you areas for growth so you can be more like Jesus. What does He show you?

We also receive conviction through others who know us well. In 1983, as the coordinator of counseling and follow-up preparing for six Billy Graham crusades in England, I met regularly with my counterpart in England, Eddie Gibbs from the Bible Society

Because we worked closely for six months, Dr. Gibbs and I spent a great deal of time together. We saw each other in a variety of situations and with many different people. We took many walks, prayed about the crusades, and became close brothers in Christ. Eddie and I have different personalities with diverse temperaments and different social skills. I am straightforward like other Americans, and Eddie is more reserved and polished. In truth, both of us were just a couple of God's kids from humble roots, seeking to walk with Christ daily in the midst of a rigorous schedule. Eddie's father was an auto mechanic, mine a carpenter.

By the end of the Crusade, we had grown to appreciate each other immensely. We committed to writing a candid letter that would detail the other's strengths and weaknesses. Each of us took time to think and pray before we wrote the letter. Today Dr. Gibbs is the Donald A. McGavran Professor of Church Growth at Fuller Theological Seminary. No matter who we are—professor, leader, auto mechanic, carpenter, homemaker—we can learn from others.

> ## *Revival is . . .*
> *God revealing Himself to men in*
> *awesome holiness and unresistable power.*
>
> —————
>
> Arthur Wallis

The Holy Spirit can also help by giving conviction through individuals. The Spirit can give us a heart to receive honest feedback from others if we are willing to relinquish that control. God may have given you tremendous strengths, but He wants you to continue to grow. So we ask the Holy Spirit to control our weaknesses and manage our strengths. Here are some steps to help with this process:

1. List your strengths as you see them. (Use the blanks below to do so.)

_____

_____

2. List your weaknesses as you see them. (Use the blanks below to do so.)

_____

_____

3. Ask a close brother or sister in Christ to evaluate your strengths and weaknesses from his or her perspective. (The same gender as you is preferable.) List the strengths and weaknesses the person mentions.

_____

_____

4. Ask God to show you ways to grow more like Him as you control your strengths and manage your weaknesses. Create a definite plan for growth with concrete goals and objectives. In the blanks below (or on a separate sheet of paper), develop and list your plan for growth.

_____

_____

_____

5. Define your spiritual plumb bobs. A plumb bob is the weight hooked beneath the tripod below a surveyor's telescope. Without this weight hanging under the center of the telescope, the surveyor cannot level the telescope. Plumb bobs give balance to your life. They often taken the form of learning and heeding the truths of Scripture.

Charlie Riggs, my spiritual mentor, always challenged me to find Scriptures that would be my "plumb bobs," which spoke to me to help balance my life. I memorized and meditated on them. For example, each day I review Ephesians 6 where Paul details our spiritual armor. By faith I prepare to face the day, putting on each piece of spiritual armor. Read Ephesians 6 now.

Over the years, this chapter has become a part of my life.

Also, plumb-bob verses give you God's Word for your various weaknesses. It might be temptation, bitterness, envy or pride, or the unwise use of the tongue or the eyes. Find the appropriate Scriptures and use them to walk each day in the conviction and power of the Holy Spirit.

Read Isaiah 55:3–8. Why is it important to seek God for conviction?

_____

_____

How is God's perspective different from our own?

_____

_____

Read Zephaniah 2:1–3. How is conviction related to salvation?

_____

_____

REVIEW THE DAY

Do you have some scriptural plumb bobs in your life? If so, write the verse references in the space below. If you've never considered this aspect of Scripture, then use Ephesians 6 as a beginning. Find one or two verses just for you.

_____

_____

Read Proverbs 11:14. Do you have someone with whom you can discuss in honesty your strengths and weaknesses? If not, write a prayer below and ask God to bring this person into your life. If you have such a friend, what have you learned from that person?

_____

_____

What was the most meaningful sentence or Bible verse in this section? Rephrase that particular sentence or verse as a prayer to God.

_____

_____

_____

What action does God want you to take as a result of today's study? Meditate, think deeply, and listen to your heart; then write about the action you will take.

_____

_____

REVIVAL TRUTHS

- God calls us to release our control and seek His conviction.
- God works through many avenues to bring conviction.
- It is better to seek conviction than have it hit you over the head.
- Scriptural plumb bobs are tools for stability.

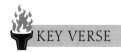

KEY VERSE

Seek ye the Lord, all ye meek of the earth, which have wrought his judgment; seek righteousness, seek meekness: it may be ye shall be hid in the day of the Lord's anger. (Zephaniah 2:3)

DAY THREE

THE ROADBLOCK
OF SIN

Many years ago, when I was in seminary, I rode in a car with a friend, discussing sin. Larry Hart, who eventually became a professor at a seminary, was driving, and I began to describe a habitual sin that affected my life. Periodically the sin would overwhelm me, I told Larry. I would repent and ask God to forgive me, but it returned again and again. This debilitating process caused me great concern, I explained.

"Tom, your problem is focusing on the sin rather than the Savior," Larry said as he continued to drive. "When you ask God to forgive you of that sin, you don't forgive yourself. He has already forgiven you, so why do you keep thinking about it? Don't focus on the sin. Focus on the Savior.

"Tom, the Bible says that Satan is a deceiver, liar, and mocker. You are letting Satan deceive you, lie to you, and mock you. God has already forgiven, and you are focusing on the sin instead of the Savior. The devil is tricking you. Don't let him do that."

That simple truth from God's Word was like a revelation. It brought a profound release unlike anything I had ever experienced and great joy flooded my heart, which exists to this day. Victory in Jesus over small or large matters is real.

I was already a Christian, but this moment changed my life. Before this point in time, I tried taking back control after repentance. The reality was, I was not in control. But God was and is. I allowed Satan to use guilt and shame to keep that sin fresh in my mind. And as that sin sat in my mind, it often led to action. I needed to treat that sin as God did, casting it away and considering it no more.

Turning from sin is important. Doing so can be painful and awkward, but it does give us freedom. We need to trust God for the forgiveness He promises. Recently a female colleague described to me the deep repentance that she and her mother had seen among women in a large city in northern California.

Almost 18,000 women listened to a speaker, Lori Graham Bakker, describe how to deal with past abortions. The shame of abortion often overrides the burden of the sin. Many women have kept silent about their sin because they feel so much condemnation from themselves and others, especially the church. Yet, God is using Lori, who has herself had five abortions, as the instrument to deliver others.[1]

Lori asked the women to respond by symbolically holding up their aborted children as an offering to the Lord. According to my colleague, an audible wailing rose from deep within their soul and spirit; it was unnatural and unnerving. Her mother turned to her and said, "I have sometimes wondered what hell sounded like. After hearing this, I never want to hear the sound of hell again."

What a burden when we've had to carry the shame of sin alone, whether from an abortion, a theft, or cruel words we later regret. We may feel the guilt of sin that has been given to God for forgiveness and yet has not been able to be aired openly. Even men are now being challenged to repent for their part in abortions.

The Lord tells us that the truth does set us free. "And ye shall know the truth, and the truth shall make you free" (John 8:32). Also, "If the Son therefore shall make you free, ye shall be free indeed" (John 8:36). For those women in northern California, giving Christ the sin in their lives removed the shame as well as the pain of taking an innocent life. There were torturous moans in the audience; yet victory was also present for all.

> *Lord of the here and now*
> *Lord of the come what may*
> *I want to believe somehow*
> *That You can heal*
> *These wounds of yesterday . . .*
> *Be the Lord of the past.*
>
> ———
>
> "LORD OF THE PAST"/Bob Bennett

Often people try to hide their guilt and shame with drugs, alcohol, isolation, overeating, or hostility. But Jesus promises release to all through His redeeming work: "The Spirit of the Lord . . . has anointed Me to preach the gospel to the poor; He has sent Me to heal the brokenhearted, to proclaim liberty to the captives, and recovery of sight to the blind, to set at liberty those who are oppressed; to proclaim the acceptable year of the Lord" (Luke 4:18–19 NKJV).

Do you still carry shame for past sins? List those sins that have left you feeling shame or guilt.

_____

_____

Make a plan to speak with someone about that shame—to request prayer for healing.

_____

_____

Consider what Paul wrote to the church at Corinth about the process of repentance in 2 Corinthians 7:9–10. Detail that process of true repentance from these verses in the space below.

_____

_____

In Luke 15:1–10, Jesus Christ told the parable of the lost sheep and the lost coin. Read this section. Note what Jesus said about the true joy derived from repentance and turning to God. Have you found this joy in your own life from repentance? If so, recount an incident briefly below.

_____

_____

REVIEW THE DAY

Have you confessed by faith and removed some areas of sin from your life? If so, list a couple of those areas below.

_____

_____

Take time to praise God for His provision through Jesus Christ. Write a brief prayer and praise below.

_____

_____

What was the most meaningful sentence or Bible verse in this section? Rephrase that particular sentence or verse as a prayer to God.

_____

_____

_____

What action does God want you to take as a result of today's study? Meditate, think deeply, and listen to your heart; then write about the action you will take.

_____

_____

REVIVAL TRUTHS

- Even confessed sin can be a roadblock if we don't receive God's forgiveness.
- Satan will try to remind us of past sins. He is a liar.
- Healing comes from accepting Jesus' death as complete atonement for our sin.

KEY VERSE

I say unto you, that likewise joy shall be in heaven over one sinner that repenteth, more than over ninety and nine just persons, which need no repentance. (Luke 15:7)

DAY FOUR

TO BE
LIKE CHRIST

Have you ever noticed that you start acting like the group of people with whom you are hanging around? Parents of teenagers are well aware of the dangers—and sometimes the benefits—of this truth. Parents want their kids to spend time with other children who hold moral and ethical values that the parents agree with, because parents know that groups of kids will act in similar ways. Otherwise, it wouldn't concern a parent if their sweet and innocent teenage girl became friends with another girl who smoked and drank and was promiscuous. It's not a given fact, but the chances are there would be some negative influence. Even adults can be prone to picking up habits, whether positive or negative, since we often develop characteristics like the people with whom we spend the most time.

Our desire should be to act like Jesus. The more time we spend with Him, the more we will be like Him. We have discussed the importance of prayer and Scripture reading, and also of practicing His presence. As we repent and turn our hearts toward Christ and away from sin, it's important to walk with Him daily.

An outstanding example of someone who walks each day with Christ, with the goal of being more like Him, is Mike MacIntosh. I first met Mike in 1976, while teaching a Christian life and witness class for the Billy Graham Crusades. We were preparing for the San Diego Crusade, and I led a class at a church filled with youth called Calvary Chapel (now called Horizon Christian Fellowship).

Pastor Mike MacIntosh was almost thirty, and he taught simply out of the Bible as he told the young listeners to follow God's Word. He gave an invitation, and scores came to the front to make decisions for Christ. To each new believer, the counselors gave a New Testament and told the new believer to go, read it, and do it. What a follow-up program, and the young followers of Christ did just that!

Afterward I met Pastor Mike, the best Bible teacher under whom I had ever sat.

He was so practical and easy to understand, and the Holy Spirit flowed through this man with such strength that he radiated Jesus.

Before coming to Christ, Mike had been a salesman and heavy drug user. A tremendous extrovert, Mike could charm almost anyone. But he owed a lot of money to the drug pushers. One day they caught Mike, put a bag over his head and shot a pistol by his ear. He was so stoned from his drug use that for many months Mike actually thought he was dead. Eventually, through the outreach of Calvary Chapel (Costa Mesa) to the southern California youth, Mike met Christ as his Lord and Savior.

In his early days of walking with Christ, Mike became the founding president of Maranatha Music, initially selling music records and tapes from the trunk of his car. Then at God's direction, he and another believer went to San Diego and started a Bible study in an apartment. Eventually this study grew into one of the fastest-growing churches in America, now named Horizon Christian Fellowship. Thousands attend each week. The church has planted more than sixty churches throughout the United States.

> *We shall not become like Christ*
> *until we give more time.*
>
> ———◆———
>
> Frank Laubach

In the beginning, Mike didn't have a college degree. Since those humble beginnings, Mike has received his undergraduate degree, two masters, and a doctorate, became a certified jet pilot and an author. Yet more important than his accomplishments, Mike is someone who humbly reflects Jesus day in and day out.

Mike MacIntosh is a good example of God's power in the life of someone who, at one time in the eyes of others, had little hope. Yet through the power of the Holy Spirit, Mike has reflected Jesus Christ to thousands because he lives in the power and joy of God's Spirit. God took Mike because of his obedience and love for the Bible and did something incredible, and it's still happening today.[2] Mike was willing to repent, to totally change his life.

How is it that Mike, who came from such a horrible place in life, can be such a clear reflection of Christ? Because Mike spends time with Christ, and he imitates what Christ does. It's not a complicated system of do's and don'ts. He also continues a lifestyle of ongoing repentance to be more like Christ.

Do you reflect Jesus in your everyday life? How do others know you want to be like Jesus? Can they see it on your face or through your actions? Write the answers to these questions below.

_____

_____

Moses spent a great deal of time with God—face to face. He spent so much time that his face began to reflect the glory of God. Read about Moses in Exodus 34:27–35. What can you learn from these verses about his relationship with God and how he reflected God?

_____

_____

The apostle Stephen also reflected Jesus in his face. Read about him in Acts 6:8–7:59. In particular, study Acts 7:55. How was Jesus reflected in Stephen?

_____

_____

How can you learn to be more like Jesus? Reading the Bible consistently? Praying more consistently? What goal can you set to be more like Jesus?

_____

_____

Meditate on these Scriptures about being more like Jesus: Romans 15:5–6 and John 5:19–20. What is the root of your relationship to be like Jesus? How can you add more of Jesus into your everyday life?

_____

_____

_____

REVIEW THE DAY

Each day you need to make a fresh commitment to grow more like Jesus. This growth flows from your love relationship. How can repentance help you to reflect Jesus more?

_____

_____

Today make a fresh commitment to grow in the knowledge of Jesus. Write a prayer with that commitment below.

_____

_____

What was the most meaningful sentence or Bible verse in this section? Rephrase that particular sentence or verse as a prayer to God.

_____

_____

_____

What action does God want you to take as a result of today's study? Meditate, think deeply, and listen to your heart; then write about the action you will take.

_____

_____

REVIVAL TRUTHS

- Through repentance in your life, you can grow more like Jesus each day.
- We are more like those with whom we spend time.

- Only by spending time daily with Christ, by knowing and obeying Him, can we be more like Him.

KEY VERSE

Now the God of patience and consolation grant you to be likeminded one toward another according to Christ Jesus: that ye may with one mind and one mouth glorify God, even the Father of our Lord Jesus Christ. (Romans 15:5–6)

DAY FIVE

FORGIVENESS

When I began my ministerial career, a Southern Baptist minister approached me and said that he knew a church of about two hundred members south of town that was looking for a pastor. In my naïveté I inquired, and eventually I became the pastor of the church. I don't know who was more naïve—them or me.

I preached vehemently every Sunday like the boy-preacher I was. On one particular communion Sunday, I admonished that the congregation shouldn't come to the altar for communion unless they had first obeyed the Scripture in Matthew 5:23–24 that said, "Therefore if thou bring thy gift to the altar, and there rememberest that thy brother hath ought against thee; leave there thy gift before the altar, and go thy way; first be reconciled to thy brother, and then come and offer thy gift." Fortunately, God used that sermon to also convict me. I realized that I too had a situation in my own life that needed attention.

"Mrs. Davis" was a godly but dominating older woman who had basically run the church. She meant well, but often spoke the truth so abrasively that it was painful to others. In a conversation with the chairman of the deacons, I mentioned my opinion about Mrs. Davis's behavior. Of course, this comment made its way to her. I realized that I was wrong and needed to make amends. I didn't want to. Mrs. Davis could be so tough; she didn't display much grace that I could see. But how could I ask others to be right before the Lord if I didn't also? I had sinned and needed to make it right with Mrs. Davis and with God.

I made my way to Mrs. Davis's house. The gate to her fence was locked, and for a moment I thought that was my escape. But conviction rose in me again, so I jumped her chain-link fence. Sheepishly approaching the back door, the entrance for friends, I rang the bell.

"Mrs. Davis, I'd like to speak with you, if you don't mind." She opened the door.

I sat down, baring my soul and the conviction God had placed on my heart about my attitude and behavior. I said that I needed to make this right before the next communion service. I asked for forgiveness.

You can imagine my shock as the tears began to roll down Mrs. Davis's face. She approached me, put her arms around me, and wept. She thanked me for my sensitivity and released the bitterness from her heart she held toward me. I was amazed.

Though not every situation ends in such a positive way, God does call us to ask for forgiveness and make amends. Perhaps the person you speak to won't offer the forgiveness you seek. That's OK. It's between that person and God. What matters is not the person's response to you, but your response in obedience to God.

> *Once we understand the depth of our sin and the distance it put between us and God and once we get a glimpse of the sacrifice God made to restore fellowship with us, we should not hesitate to get involved in the process of forgiveness.*
>
> ---
>
> Charles Stanley

Read Matthew 18:21–35. Why are we expected to forgive others?

_____

_____

What is God's response to those who do not forgive?

_____

_____

Read Ephesians 4:30–32. Unforgiveness can lead to bitterness, rage, and anger. It grieves God to see His children fighting against each other. Is there someone who has offended you and has not asked for forgiveness? List the person and the offense. Make a plan to speak with this person—to make things right.

_____

_____

REVIEW THE DAY

Is there someone you have sinned against? Describe the situation.

_____

_____

Make a plan to ask for forgiveness.

_____

_____

What will you do if the person refuses to forgive you?

_____

_____

What was the most meaningful thought or Bible verse in this section? Rephrase that particular thought or verse as a prayer to God.

_____

_____

_____

What action does God want you to take as a result of today's study? Meditate, think deeply, and listen to your heart; then write about the action you will take.

_____

_____

_____

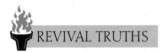

REVIVAL TRUTHS

- God calls us to confess our sins to others and to ask for forgiveness.
- We are called to make any amends necessary for damage repair.
- The other person's response is not up to us; our obedience to God is what counts.

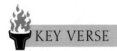

KEY VERSE

Jesus saith unto him, I say not unto thee, until seven times: but, until seventy times seven. (Matthew 18:22)

LOOKING AHEAD

Repentance requires a determination to turn completely away from anything not of God. Though modern believers often see repentance as punishment, it is a normal and healthy part of our relationship with God and others. Without repentance, there can be no forgiveness, and without forgiveness, there can be no salvation. Without salvation, there can be no revival. In chapter 4 we will look at the role obedience plays in revival.

4 OBEDIENCE

In the work of God worldwide, there are many unsung heroes. Mark Buntain is a great example. In 1954 Mark and Huldah Buntain went for a six-month missionary trip to Calcutta, India. They rented a small apartment for their short stay. Thirty-four years later, the Buntains were living in the same apartment. During the short-term trip, they heard God's call to stay in India. They obeyed.

Starting from an upstairs hall they built a ministry compound, *Calcutta Mission of Mercy*, with a preaching facility that would seat 1,500 and a 167-bed teaching hospital that would welcome doctors, nurses, interns, and doctors in residence. Before Mark Buntain's death on June 4, 1989, they were feeding and teaching more than 10,000 children each day.[1] Today Huldah continues to run this work, which is just around the corner from the ministry that had been run by Mother Teresa, a close friend of the mission. Mark's obedience to God is a model of obedience to God's call and direction.

Once an American reporter was in the streets of Calcutta and saw a man sitting hunched on the concrete sidewalk, leaning against a wall. The reporter was a Christian, and the Lord impressed him to speak to the man about Jesus. He asked, "Do you know God?"

"Yes, I do. In fact, I've met him, and God will be here in the morning."

"Really?" the reporter said with a bemused look on his face.

OBEDIENCE

"Yes; do you want to meet him? Well, meet me here at 6 A.M., and I'll show you God."

The next morning, the reporter came to the spot. He didn't expect the old man to be there, thinking it was probably a joke. But the same man was waiting and said, "Come with me." At first, they began walking down a fairly wide street in the city, but, as they continued, the street began to narrow. Finally they were walking in the poor section of Calcutta with tiny walkways of dirt and running sewage between shack homes. As they wound through a maze of humanity, suddenly they turned into a small courtyard. Standing in the middle of the courtyard was Mark Buntain and his associates, who were passing out bread to the poor.

The old man pointed and said, "See, there's God." Through Mark's obedience to the Savior, he made a profound impression on the people of India about the love of Jesus Christ.[2]

God may not be calling you to India, but He does call you to obey in your daily life. Most people are almost as uncomfortable with the word *obedience* as they are with the word *repentance*. Yet obedience is foundational to rekindle your fire and to bring about revival. For the next five days let's explore the role of obedience in personal revival.

DAY ONE

THE CALL TO OBEY
GOD'S WORD—HOLINESS

England's great revival in the mid-1700s started with an unlikely group of three young men who began a club to pursue spiritual disciplines in the midst of their theological education. In 1729 Charles Wesley and two other students began to meet weekly to discuss the subjects of a holy life. They started their meetings with prayer, studied the New Testament and Christian books, reviewed what they were going to do that day, and planned the next. Often they would meet again for supper. This desire to be holy grew until the group was called the "Holy Club."

The three men lived by stringent rules and had a method of:

- daily self-examination
- prayer
- weekly communion
- fasting on Wednesdays and Fridays—an imitation of the early church
- meditating on different days on topics such as "The Love of God in Simplicity," "The Love of Man," etc.

In addition, the three members of the Holy Club sought God's will in everything. They strove each day to develop a virtue such as humility or faith, and each day at 9, 12 and 3 o'clock they repeated the printed prayers of the Church of England. They soon were joined by others, including Charles's older brother John, who years earlier had been a devout student while studying at Christ Church College in Oxford; there he earned his master's degree in 1727. John soon became the accepted leader of the group. Eventually, for their systematic approach, they were called, in derision, the "Methodists."

They visited jails, teaching the prisoners to read and pray. They visited the sick.

The Holy Club never exceeded twenty-five in number because such discipline deterred others. They assisted poor families and poor children, teaching them to read.[3]

Out of these desires, God turned them into men who would realize that the disciplines were effectual only through a personal relationship with Jesus Christ. As John Wesley would later write in his journal, "I've come to convert the heathen, but, oh, who will convert me?" Then his heart was strangely touched at a meeting one evening where the preface to the book of Romans was being read; he noted of that occasion, "I felt my heart strangely warmed."

> *In revival, holiness becomes a constant necessity, rather than an occasional option.*
>
> Mark Stibbe

The Church of England had become an institution. It did not promote the spiritual side of life described in the books John, Charles, George Whitfield, and the others began to read. But these men yearned for this personal relationship with Christ. And the Lord honored their seeking, as He promises He will. Through these committed young men of "methods," the church of Jesus Christ began to grow.

What an example of obedience. The sacrifices were overwhelming. History records that even when they preached in the open-air meetings, rocks, broken glass, punches, or even dead cats were hurled at them. Mobs who were offended by the simple proclamation of the Gospel often attacked them and their followers, once even shredding John Wesley's clothes. But God was preeminent. He worked through key men who, within the Church of England, were nobodies. Yet, God raised them up to do His will in bringing revival.[4]

As we look at our nation today, it's important to consider the disciplines of a holy life of obedience. These young men sought an intimate walk with Christ through obedience and a nation was changed. They were obedient regardless of the consequences.

Are you willing to do that today—to obey God regardless of the consequences? Write your response to that question.

Read 2 Timothy 1:8–12. How is it that we can live a holy life?

_____

_____

Use your concordance and look up other references to the word _holy_. What does it mean?

_____

_____

How are holiness and obedience related? Read Romans 12:1–2. Why is being "a living sacrifice" the "least we can do"? Why does such sacrifice please God?

_____

_____

Perhaps God is not asking you to change an entire nation. Perhaps He is calling you to change one aspect of your life. Are you willing to step out in faith and obey? Record your response.

_____

_____

REVIEW THE DAY

Read 1 Corinthians 9:24–27. Why is obedience critical for revival?

_____

_____

Pray now that God would help you identify and stand against anything that stands in the way of your obedience to Him. Record that prayer.

_____

_____

OBEDIENCE

What was the most meaningful sentence or Bible verse in this section? Rephrase that particular sentence or verse as a prayer to God.

_____

_____

REVIVAL TRUTHS

- God uses ordinary people, willing to obey and live holy lives, to make great changes.
- We are all called to a life of holy obedience.
- We must be willing to obey no matter what the cost.

KEY VERSE

But I keep under my body, and bring it into subjection: lest that by any means, when I have preached to others, I myself should be a castaway. (1 Corinthians 9:27)

DAY TWO

OBEDIENCE IN THE SMALL THINGS

Charlie Riggs, my spiritual mentor, used to say, "Small things are those from which large things flow." My mother believed that truth before I ever heard Charlie say it. As a sort of "forewoman" at a local factory, she observed many workers pulling discarded items from the garbage can. These items were genuine discards from the plant, such as old rolls of wire or small pincher pliers with a piece of the point broken off. These items were no longer usable at the factory but could possibly be used at a worker's home. My mother determined these items didn't belong to her, and she would not take them.

As a little boy walking along the street, I found a dollar bill. In my day, that bill was a tremendous amount of money, and I wanted to pick it up. Mother said, "Tom, leave it."

With a questioning tone, I echoed, "Leave it? Somebody lost this dollar, and they don't know where they lost it."

"Son, you don't know that they don't know where they lost this dollar. Whoever lost this money knows where they have been today and they may retrace their steps to try and locate it. It may be very important to them. You must leave it. It's not yours."

As a child, that money was important, so I tried one more time. "But, Mom, it doesn't matter. It's lost. The next guy will pick it up."

"Tom, God sees you every moment of every day, and that money is not yours. The point is ownership, so don't pick it up." Through a practical (and painful!) example, my mother was teaching that little things grow into big things. The big things in life are made out of small choices. Big obedience comes from small steps of obedience. If you open the disobedience window, then you allow the cancerous growth of disobedience to begin in your life.

93

OBEDIENCE

> *Purify my heart,*
> *Let me be as gold and precious silver.*
>
> ———◆———
>
> "REFINER'S FIRE"/Brian Doerksen

Once, as the director of the 1987 Denver Billy Graham Crusade, I drove Dr. Graham to some appointments a few days before the Crusade. The speed limit was 55 miles per hour, and I was driving between 62 and 64 mph. Dr. Graham turned to me and asked, "Tom, do you believe in obeying the speed limit?"

I stammered, "Well . . . yes," as I looked at my speedometer.

Dr. Graham continued. "I believe in obeying the law. The Bible says render unto Caesar the things that are Caesar's and unto God the things that are God's. I just don't speed. I don't think God can honor you when you are speeding."

Of course, before he had finished his explanation, my speed slowed to 55 mph, my face was flushed, and I was a little saint driving with my halo over the driver's seat. To this day, it impressed me how much Billy Graham cared about obeying the law. These little aspects of life are the building blocks of obedience.

Jesus told the parable of the talents in Matthew 25:14–30. Reread this parable, then remember that in terms of talent, the Lord is asking us to use what we have for the kingdom. If we have little, then we should use it faithfully, and God will give more. Jesus concludes His parable with the profound statement, "For unto every one that hath shall be given, and he shall have abundance: but from him that hath not shall be taken away even that which he hath" (Matthew 25:29). It is the same with obedience. If we can be faithful in the small, painless areas of life, God can trust us with more.

How does the parable in Matthew 25 apply to your life? In your relationship with God?

_____

_____

In what small area can you give more in obedience?

_____

_____

94

Honesty is an area that has become particularly gray. We find many ways to avoid the whole truth. We keep secrets. We make promises and don't keep them. Read Acts 5:1–11 and notice the example of Ananias and Sapphira, his wife. They sold some land then supposedly gave the money to the church, but lied about the actual sale price. The apostle Peter, speaking in the power of the Holy Spirit, pointed out their lies and each died instantly. Their story was an example to the early Church and also to us. Each day we need to live honestly before the Lord. We also see from this example that when there is a choice between obeying God or obeying man, perhaps as in the case of Sapphira, it's best to obey God.

Do you feel you are an honest person? Why or why not?

_____

_____

Read Proverbs 16:11 and 20:23 and explain our need for balance in our treatment of other people.

_____

_____

Pray now that God would reveal to you any dishonesty in your heart. Record God's response.

_____

_____

God calls us to be faithful with the small aspects of life, and that involves our consistent obedience to the Lord.

REVIEW THE DAY

James 3:3 describes how riders place bits in horses' mouths so they will obey. Read that first portion of James 3; then consider whether you are willing for God to put His bit of truth in your mouth. What is your response to God's call to obey His commands?

_____

_____

Evaluate your response to the commands in God's Word. (Are you reading the Word of God enough to know truth and to know how to obey Him?) Are you willing to give up your traditions or biases whenever you come across God's truths? If so, write a brief prayer of commitment below.

_____

_____

Hebrews 5:9 reveals one important aspect of obedience. Salvation comes to all who obey. We have to take some steps in obedience to come to know Christ. What steps do you need to take to increase your obedience?

_____

_____

What was the most meaningful sentence or Bible verse in this section? Rephrase that particular sentence or verse as a prayer to God.

_____

_____

_____

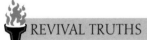

REVIVAL TRUTHS

- Obedience is a matter of faithfulness—with the small and large aspects of life.
- There is no area too small or too large to ignore God's call to obedience.

KEY VERSE

And being made perfect, he became the author of eternal salvation unto all them that obey him. (Hebrews 5:9)

DAY THREE

OBEDIENCE IN YOUR RELATIONSHIPS

To rekindle the spiritual fire in your life, you must be in right relationship with God, yourself, and others. If any one of these relationships is out of balance, it's difficult to rekindle your fire. We have to remove anything in the way that hinders the love between God and us.

As a child, "Sheila" had been molested by a woman claiming to be a friend of the family. The molestation continued for about two years, until Sheila was twelve years old. Though they attended church, Sheila's own family neglected her, which opened the door for the abuse. It became difficult for this little girl to separate love from sex. Though she was being molested, her perpetrator was kind and nurturing—giving all that Sheila lacked in her own home.

> *I'm trading my sorrow.*
> *I'm trading my shame.*
> *I'm laying them down*
> *For the sake of the Lord.*
>
> ———
>
> "TRADING MY SORROWS"/Darrell Evans

When Sheila became a young adult, she entered into a sexual relationship with another woman. She knew it was not pleasing to God, but felt it was what she deserved. It was love, after all, she told herself. Yet she was not at peace about her life and began to seek God. In the process of seeking, she realized that to ever be free from the anguish that bound her, Sheila would have to walk away from the only caring relationship she knew. She had to obey God in having relationships that honored Him, and allow Him to work in her life. Sheila left the sinful relationship and found peace as she continued to seek God's love.

Perhaps you are in a relationship that is damaging to you. It may be a sexual relationship outside of marriage. Or it may be a friendship with someone who influences you away from God. Any relationship that distracts your attention from God is not pleasing to Him.

Think about the relationships in your life. Do they encourage you to walk more closely with God? Are there any that are damaging to you? Write your response.

_____

_____

Is there any relationship that God is calling you to leave? Or is there one He asks you to work through to repair? What's the difference?

_____

_____

Conversely, God may be calling you *into* a relationship. Perhaps He has shown you someone who is lonely or needy. Perhaps He has asked you to extend your hand of friendship, to walk through a difficult time with another. Just as He calls us to leave some relationships, He calls us to enter into others.

Read 1 Corinthians 12:21–26. What is our responsibility to others in the body of Christ?

_____

_____

Ask God to bring to mind anyone to whom He has called you to reach out. Make a plan to do so.

_____

_____

Read Mark 11:25. Most people have been wounded in some way. It is common to carry anger or unforgiveness against those who hurt us. But this is not God's plan. Pray now. Ask God to bring to mind any unforgiveness you carry against someone else. Has He brought any situation to mind?

_____

_____

Confess to God that you forgive this person for the offense. Does God ask you to do anything else with regard to this situation?

_____

_____

Scripture gives us pictures of healthy relationships. Just as we can be in an unhealthy relationship, God wants us to care for the relationships to which He has called us. If you are married, are there areas that need attention in that relationship to make it more honoring to God? Describe that. If you are *not* married, what relationships has God specifically called you to? How can you better tend to those relationships?

_____

_____

We are called into relationship in the body. If you feel isolated, ask God to show you areas in your life that may keep you from developing close relationships with others. Record those, and make a plan to battle those areas.

_____

_____

_____

REVIEW THE DAY

One of the most well-defined friendships in the Bible was that between David and Jonathan. Read 1 Samuel 18–20. What characterized their friendship and what can you learn about relationships from their example?

_____

_____

Today make a new commitment to be in synch on your relationships with God, self, and others. Write a prayer with that commitment below.

_____

_____

What was the most meaningful sentence or Bible verse in this section? Rephrase that particular sentence or verse as a prayer to God.

_____

_____

_____

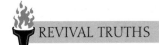

REVIVAL TRUTHS

- In obedience to the Lord, our relationships with God, self, and others need to be constantly growing and improving.
- We need to realize sinful relationships will hinder God's work in our lives.
- God calls us to forgive others and keep unhindered relationships with other members of the body.
- God wants us to care for the relationships with which He has blessed us.

KEY VERSE

Then Jonathan and David made a covenant, because he loved him as his own soul. (1 Samuel 18:3 NKJV)

DAY FOUR

OBEDIENCE IN YOUR CALLING

In 1 Corinthians 12, the apostle Paul wrote about the interdependence of the body of Christ. In verse 18, Paul declared, "But now hath God set the members every one of them in the body, as it hath pleased him." Because of our uniqueness, God gives us each a different calling in life. Though we are all called to share the Gospel and minister to others, we do it differently.

Some are called to full-time Christian service as both a mission calling and as a vocation. This requires obedience. I wanted to be a doctor. I knew I was skilled to become a doctor. I saw an opportunity to serve God as a doctor. God wanted me instead to be in a preaching ministry full time. I had to make a choice of obedience to follow where He led rather than where I thought was a good place to go.

Others are called to a "secular" vocation, to serve God daily among the lost and hurting of the world. Such ministry also requires obedience. Susan, a young woman who loves the Lord, has an intense desire to go overseas as a missionary. For the time being, at least, God has called her to work in an office environment, to be Jesus to those around her each day. Before you get the wrong idea, God does not immediately call us to the exact opposite of what we desire! I use Susan and myself simply as examples of being obedient wherever God's call may lead.

If you are not full-time clergy, it's tempting to think that it's someone else's job to do the ministry. After all, the professionals get paid to do it. There is also a temptation for those in church, parachurch, and missions ministries to see themselves as more "holy" or "special" than those who serve elsewhere. In truth, we are all in ministry to others as we serve the Father. As we will discuss in Chapter 7, often the difference between sacred and secular is the attitude with which the work is done, not the work itself. What matters is our obedience.

God has called each of us to be ministers of the Gospel: We are His ambassadors (2 Corinthians 5:20) wherever we work—in the law office, on a construction crew, on an oil rig off the coast of Alaska, or working in a military installation. It's important to realize:

- God made us.
- God created us as His children through His Son.
- God has a plan for our lives.
- As we are disciplined, obedient, and pure, He will put that plan into practice in our lives.
- He made us as a piece of the mosaic. When we follow Him, He supernaturally puts us in His big picture of ministry, which can change the world if we are all faithful.

> *Revival, in its fullness, will see neighborhoods,*
> *schools, workplaces and cultures*
> *changed and healed.*
>
> Mark DuPont

Obedience in our vocation and calling means: (1) remembering that He sees us every moment, (2) wanting to please Him, (3) having a relationship with Him that makes pleasing Him naturally fulfilling, (4) being available through purity of heart in obedience to do what He has called us to do each day, and (5) being sensitive to His Spirit and asking Him to guide us to what He has in store for us that day.

When Ouida and I first came to Colorado Springs, we met Ann, a real-estate agent recommended to us. Ann was seeking spiritually and exploring New Age philosophies. Ouida and I instantly liked her. As we drove around viewing homes, Ann discovered that I had been working for Billy Graham. This was intriguing. Then Ann found out I was writing a book. I didn't know exactly how to tell her about the subject, revival, and I didn't want to use that word because I didn't know what connotations she might draw.

So I said, "It's a book about spiritual life."

"Well," she said, "spiritual life. I'm into spiritual life. What's it all about?"

I began to tell her about how God could be a part of her life and bring tremendous fulfillment and joy. Then from that spiritual connection would come a balanced individual who can be successful, with God's help. I got her a copy of the book when it was published, and our relationship continued to grow. Three and a half years later, my wife had the privilege of helping Ann come to a personal relationship with Christ.

Today, both Ann and her husband are faithful worshipers and growing in the Lord. Recently Ann told us, "You will never know how much it means to us that Ouida and you guided us to God." I was being obedient by following God's call to move to Colorado for a new ministry job. Ouida was following her call as my wife. Through this obedience, we were in the right place at the right time to minister to someone God brought to us. Through obedience in our calling, we can change the lives of people who cross our path.

REVIEW THE DAY

Study the prayer that Paul wrote in 2 Thessalonians 1:11–12. What insight do you gain about your work and the relationship to God in your life from these verses? Write your insight below.

_____

_____

Read Psalm 62:12. How are you using your occupation in obedience to God? What can you do to better use your occupation or work for God's work?

_____

_____

In 2 Thessalonians 3:1–10, Paul wrote about how he worked for his food and wasn't a burden on those people who received his ministry. What application can you receive from these verses for your own life and work?

_____

_____

OBEDIENCE

Today make a fresh commitment to use your occupation in obedience to God. Write a prayer with that commitment below.

_____

_____

What was the most meaningful sentence or Bible verse in this section? Rephrase that particular sentence or verse as a prayer to God.

_____

_____

_____

REVIVAL TRUTHS

- Our vocation or calling (no matter what) is to serve in obedience to the Lord.
- Our work is secular or sacred only in attitude, not in the work itself.
- God can use us to change the lives of others if we are obedient.

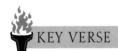

KEY VERSE

Also unto thee, O Lord, belongeth mercy: for thou renderest to every man according to his work. (Psalm 62:12)

DAY FIVE

OBEDIENCE UNTIL DEATH

As growing young Christians, a group of us were asked the question, "Would you be willing to die for Jesus?" Immediately, many responded "Yes!" Perhaps it was easy to respond in the affirmative because we never thought that we'd actually be called to go through with it. Or perhaps we didn't understand death.

As I grew older, I began to realize that though dying for Jesus could mean a physical sacrifice, it also meant giving up any rights to a life I thought I wanted to own. There are two ways to obey Christ until death: one is a literal physical death, and the other is to lose our lives in order to find them in Jesus.

As a young man with a promising future, Jim Elliot heard God's call to the jungle. Many around Jim feared that he was throwing away his life, that he should stay home and stir up the church in America. In his diary, on his first trip to Ecuador, Jim wrote, "My going to Ecuador is God's counsel, as is my leaving Betty [at the home base], and my refusal to be counseled by all who insist I should stay and stir up the believers in the U.S."[5]

Jim felt it more important to pursue that to which God called, rather than live a life of comfort in the United States. On the wall of his primitive hut was a sign that read: *You have to go out, but you don't have to come back.* In January 1956, Auca Indians murdered Jim Elliot and four other missionaries.

Was there something unusual about Jim? No, not other than his hunger for God. Jim was willing to follow the words of Luke 9:23–24.

Read those verses in Luke now and summarize them.

_____

_____

Are you willing to daily die to yourself to follow Christ? Explain your response.

_____

_____

Why does it sometimes seem more difficult to live for Christ than to die for Him?

_____

_____

> *You have to go out,*
> *but you don't have to come back.*
>
> ———❖———
>
> SIGN IN THE HUT OF MISSIONARY JIM ELLIOT

Another of the missionaries was Pete Fleming. In preparation for working with the Aucas, Pete also kept a diary. Pete understood that though life was precious, it was worth dying to see others come to the saving knowledge of Christ. In his diary Pete wrote, "I am longing now to reach the Aucas if God gives me the honor of proclaiming the Name among them. . . . I would gladly give my life for that tribe if only to see an assembly of those proud, clever, smart people gathering around a table to honor the Son—gladly, gladly, gladly! What more could be given to a life?"[6] Only a few short years later, Pete, Jim , and the other three missionaries would be dead.

What brought about the love and devotion of these men for a people they hadn't yet met? They prayed. They walked with God intimately. They sought a life of purity and obedience. They realized the owner of their lives was God, and not them. With that, they were able to die to Christ as they lived, and live with Christ as they died.

For most people reading this, God hasn't called you to a foreign country to die as a martyr. He has, however, called you to give Him complete control over your life.

Are there areas of your life that you try to take control from God? List them. Then pray that God would make you willing to surrender every aspect of your life to Him.

_____

_____

Read Isaiah 51:6. Why is this truth important to remember as you obey Christ?

_____

_____

REVIEW THE DAY

Today make a fresh commitment to obey God in life until death. Write a prayer with that commitment below.

_____

_____

What was the most meaningful sentence or Bible verse in this section? Rephrase that particular sentence or verse as a prayer to God.

_____

_____

_____

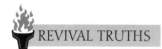

REVIVAL TRUTHS

- God calls us to obey Him even until death.
- We can die to ourselves even while we are still alive on earth.

KEY VERSE

Lift up your eyes to the heavens, and look on the earth beneath. For the heavens will vanish away like smoke, the earth will grow old like a garment, and those who dwell in it will die in like manner; but My salvation will be forever, and My righteousness will not be abolished. (Isaiah 51:6 NKJV)

OBEDIENCE

| LOOKING AHEAD |

Obedience is a daily dying to our wills and desires as we follow God wherever He leads. Sometimes we are called to physically die out of obedience, but more often we are called to live in obedience. Next week we'll see how living an obedient life opens the gates for communication through prayer.

5 PRAYER

What is prayer? The answer initially may seem obvious. Yet Jesus' disciples had already lived with Him for several years when they said, "Lord, teach us to pray" (Luke 11:1). They didn't ask, "Lord, teach us to witness"—even though they believed in evangelism. They didn't ask, "Lord, teach us to study the Scriptures"—even though they knew that was important. These disciples looked at the life of Jesus and identified the core of His relationship with His Father, so they asked Jesus to teach them to pray.

Prayer is two-way communication, and an obvious outpouring of the Holy Spirit comes from concerted and united prayer. E.M. Bounds noted that "God gives Himself to the praying ones, and that the measure of God's revelation to the soul is proportionate to the soul's longing, importunate prayer for God. Salvation never finds its way to a prayerless heart. The Holy Spirit never abides in a prayerless spirit. . . . Christ knows nothing of prayerless Christians."[1]

Just as human relationships require constant connection through communication, our relationship with God needs and deserves the same. We cannot grow in our relationship with God apart from speaking to and hearing from Him. It's this depth in relationship that will lead to both personal and corporate revival.

DAY ONE

PRAYER AS COMMUNICATION

Prayer is a simple means of communication. It began with Adam in the garden. When God first spoke with Adam and Eve, communication flowed unhindered from both directions. Those were the first prayers. After Adam and Eve sinned, prayer became more of a spiritual discipline. Communication with God was now less direct, without seeing God face to face, but it still happened.

Prayer is nothing more than a spiritual continuation of God's face-to-face contact with Adam and Eve in the garden. Look at this conversation:

> And they heard the sound of the Lord God walking in the garden in the cool of the day, and Adam and his wife hid themselves from the presence of the Lord God among the trees of the garden. Then the Lord God called to Adam and said to him, "Where are you?" So he said, "I heard Your voice in the garden, and I was afraid because I was naked; and I hid myself" (Genesis 3:8–10 NKJV).

Sin entered the picture and became a barrier to communication. It will be important for you to focus on dealing with sin as you read chapter 5. Sin brought shame, so Adam and Eve hid. Prayer is a way to keep us before God, to keep us from hiding.

In Laconia, Indiana, a small agricultural community across the Ohio River from Louisville, Kentucky, Richard had been the known "druggie" for years. Then, at age seventeen, he made a commitment to Christ. He quickly became a spiritual firebrand and witnessed door to door, seemingly every day. This young man would even visit different churches and challenge pastors right in the middle of their messages.

At the time, I was a twenty-two year old, a full-time seminary student in Louisville, and part-time pastor in Laconia. I considered Richard a bit of a nuisance.

Thankfully, he never interrupted me. But one day Richard did approach me and asked, "Brother Tom, do you pray an hour a day?"

With regret, I answered, "No."

Then he confided how he prayed an hour a day on his knees in his bedroom after high school before witnessing. He said, "I could never have the courage to go out and talk with people about Christ unless I prayed an hour a day. I challenge you to spend an hour a day in prayer."

Richard's challenge seemed impossible. My days were filled. I managed a group of maintenance men for about 1,500 apartments, in five complexes, throughout the south side of Louisville. In addition to this full-time job, I took a full course load at seminary and pastored the church. In the basement of our rented old farmhouse, I studied each day late into the night. In the midst of that crowded schedule, I made a little time for my wife and our small daughter, Cara.

But I took this young man's challenge seriously and began to pray. Usually right before midnight I would stop studying to begin praying for an hour. I started on my knees with a prayer list, then listened in silence for God to speak.

> *Prayer is both one of the means and one of the fruits of union with Christ.*
>
> Andrew Murray

One evening after supper, Ouida and I had another argument, and I stormed off to the basement to study. I could hear Ouida vacuuming loudly overhead and knew she was angry. In my prayers that night, I talked with God about our arguing. I was trying to justify myself before God by saying things like, "Lord, she's such a nag . . . "

Suddenly His voice came into my mind, telling me to be quiet. That voice spoke with authority and urgency.

I protested and wanted to argue with God at first. But then I heard His voice, shouting, "Shut up!"

After a few minutes of silence I said, "OK, Lord, now I've shut up. What do you have to say?" How arrogant I was!

My mind was flooded with Bible verses from God that asked me if I had been my family's prophet, priest, and king. Was I leading them spiritually? As I considered the question, I knew I was partially at fault. Then I inquired in prayer, "God, how much am I at fault?" Clearly I was battling with pride. It was important for me to be right and win an argument—with Ouida or God.

The answer was clear: "100 percent."

That night I was a broken young man as I yielded my marriage to God. Tears flowed down my cheeks as I admitted my accountability to God for my marriage and my 100 percent responsibility as the husband and father. Prayer made me open to God's guidance. It wasn't a one-way diatribe. It was communication from me to God, and more importantly, from God to me. The challenge from the young man saved my marriage and changed my prayer life.

REVIEW THE DAY

Examine your own life of prayer. How much time during the day do you spend in concerted prayer? Do you feel it is sufficient?

_____

_____

Identify your barriers to prayer. Do you have a plan to overcome them? What is it?

_____

_____

Read Psalm 20. What are the benefits of prayer?

_____

_____

Jesus prayed all night in Luke 6:12 and the next day He chose the various disciples. What conclusion can you draw about the place of prayer in Christ's daily life?

_____

_____

PRAYER

Today make a fresh commitment to increase prayer in your life. Write a prayer with that commitment below.

_____

_____

_____

What was the most meaningful sentence or Bible verse in this section? Rephrase that particular sentence or verse as a prayer to God.

_____

_____

_____

REVIVAL TRUTHS

- Prayer is simply communication with our heavenly Father.
- With conscious effort we can increase the amount of time we spend in prayer.
- God cannot change us if we hide from Him by not praying.

KEY VERSE

May He grant you according to your heart's desire, and fulfill all your purpose. (Psalm 20:4 NKJV)

DAY TWO

A CLEAN HEART

I've noticed that people are different in how they define the word *clean*, especially when it comes to their homes. Some people think their house is clean when they've dusted and vacuumed, yet never notice the stacks of newspapers, knick-knacks, ancient magazines, or other clutter in their house. They may have TV-dinner trays stacked on the kitchen counter—just in case they need them. Other people haven't dusted their house in years, but have wide-open floor space for the dust bunnies to roam because there is no clutter. I think both of these terms, *clutter* and *clean*, are important to consider when examining the cleanliness of our hearts.

Read Psalm 51:10. David realized the value of an unhindered movement of God's spirit in his heart, and that unhindered movement required a pure heart. You can't purify your own heart. It's only through God that you can receive such cleansing. That is why prayer is so important.

Sin is like the dirty house. There is dust covering everything. The carpet needs to be vacuumed and the trash removed. Prayer offers a time for you to confess your sins to God and for Him to forgive you. God wants to speak to you, but God's voice is difficult to hear if it is hindered by sin.

Take time now and pray. Ask God to reveal to you any area of your heart that is unclean. Perhaps you have unresolved anger or bitterness. Perhaps your thought life is not pleasing to God. Pray now and ask Him to reveal those areas to you, and ask for His forgiveness. It is important to incorporate times like this into your daily prayer life. It's also important to be open to hearing God speak about these issues even as they occur throughout the day. In the blank below, make a note of what God is saying to you about these issues.

> *Create in me a clean heart, O God,*
> *and renew a right spirit within me.*
>
> ———◆———
>
> PSALM 51:10

Our heart can also be cluttered. Maybe there isn't "sin" in the way we normally consider sin, but maybe our lives are full of clutter or the noises of life that hinders our communication with God. If you allow your busy life to prevent you from taking time to kneel before the Lord on a daily basis, when does He have the opportunity to speak to you?

The great prophet Elijah searched for God's voice in 1 Kings 19:11–12, and He heard God saying, "Go out, and stand on the mountain before the Lord." The Scriptures report that the Lord passed by, and a fierce wind raced into the mountains, breaking many rocks, "but the Lord was not in the wind; and after the wind an earthquake, but the Lord was not in the earthquake; and after the earthquake a fire, but the Lord was not in the fire; and after the fire a still small voice" (NKJV). The prophet heard God in the still small voice. With the noise in our world, it takes a commitment through prayer to hear God's voice.

Thoughts in Solitude by Thomas Merton is a valuable book to help us understand the value of solitude and time alone with God. We learn about such aspects as solitude's simplicity, and the silence of solitude through which the quiet voice of God comes booming.

Yesterday I described how young Richard challenged me to pray an hour daily, in spite of a full life. Before you think my system for prayer was that of a spiritual person with no concerns, let me share that I had a serious problem during that time. Besides my duties as a pastor, maintenance man, and seminary student, my marriage needed attention. It was in terrible shape because I hadn't been hearing from God. I couldn't hear from God properly as long as arrogance and egotism and self-righteousness dominated my heart. These factors were dirt and clutter that hindered my relationship with God and my family.

How did I experience a breakthrough? It came from discipline over a six-month period of praying for an hour at the end of each long day. Those midnight until 1A.M. prayer times were a discipline, but that's when God spoke to me.

Discipline to most is foreign, something that people often see as legalistic in our culture. Some people are disciplined about particular aspects of their lives. I have friends who golf on certain days each week. That's a discipline. Other friends fast one day a week. That's a different discipline. Each of us knows people who have a daily quiet time with God. That's another discipline. We have to discipline our tongue not to speak profanity or discipline our minds not to think evil of others. Discipline is a choice, a decision, and prayer is a discipline.

Read Psalm 139. If God already knows our innermost being, why pray?

_____

_____

In order to hear God, we must listen to Him as part of our prayer time. Why is this difficult?

_____

_____

REVIEW THE DAY

Pray again for God to reveal to you any further sin. Confess that sin. Listen for God to speak. Make a note of what God is teaching you through this prayer time.

_____

_____

What clutters your life and makes it difficult for you to pray? List those items. What will you do to remove the clutter?

_____

_____

What is your concept of discipline in prayer? How does your view of discipline align with that in God's Word, as seen in 1 Corinthians 9:23–27?

_____

_____

Today make a fresh commitment to increase your prayer life. Write a prayer with that commitment below.

_____

_____

What was the most meaningful sentence or Bible verse in this section? Rephrase that particular sentence or verse as a prayer to God.

_____

_____

_____

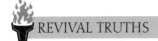

REVIVAL TRUTHS

- Our hearts can be unclean by either dirt (sin) or clutter.
- We cannot hear God speak through an unclean heart.
- Discipline is required to continually come before God and ask Him to reveal to us our sin.

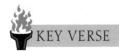

KEY VERSE

Search me, O God, and know my heart: try me, and know my thoughts: and see if there be any wicked way in me, and lead me in the way everlasting. (Psalm 139:23–24)

DAY THREE

MORE THAN
ONE WAY TO PRAY

Newsweek had an interesting front-cover headline on its January 6, 1992, issue: "Talking to God, An Intimate Look at the Way We Pray." The cover story revealed, "More than three quarters (78%) of all Americans pray at least once a week; more than half (57%) pray at least once a day."

Although the quality and depth of their prayers were unknown, apparently Americans recognized the need for prayer. "Prayer is the fundamental way we relate to God," Father Thomas Keating told the *Newsweek* reporter. Keating, a Trappist monk at St. Benedict's Monastery in Snowmass, Colorado, spends six months of every year teaching laymen and laywomen the techniques of silent, contemplative prayer. "Like any relationship it goes through stages, from acquaintance to friendliness, then on to friendship, love and finally union," he explained.[2]

Prayer is communication with our heavenly Father. In a child-and-father relationship, it is well for a child to speak but wiser still for a child to listen when he or she is in the presence of the Father. Much can be said in a Christian's life, but how much better for God to do most of the speaking. Yet by what means do we increase our time and quality of prayer? Is there only one way to pray? Just as communication between people differs as relationships and circumstances differ, so does prayer with our heavenly Father. There are several different means to prayer.

First, you can be in solitude and alone before God. This discipline is the primary way you speak to Him, and a way for you to quiet your heart and listen.

Read Mark 1:35 and John 6:15. What was Jesus' example of prayer?

_____

_____

Second, you can pray with one or more accountability partners with whom you meet periodically. In chapter 2, I introduced you to Joe Leininger, my accountability partner. We meet periodically to talk, walk, and pray together. Everyone needs this type of accountability partner. Often this accountability partner is your spouse but if not, then a same-gender accountability partner is recommended.

In *A Time to Pray,* Evelyn Christenson mentions that praying together with others, with triplets of Christians, was common in the Bible. Peter, James, and John were the triplet group when Christ prayed. Christ thought so highly of this group He asked them to pray with Him prior to His arrest. Christenson rightly notes that ". . . a threefold cord is not quickly broken." (Ecclesiastes 4:12b). Evelyn noted six benefits of praying together. Such prayer:

- forces a convenient location
- does not require expense, as these would be our friends who live close by us
- can be accomplished in just a few minutes a week
- has the accountability of others praying with you
- encourages joy rather than weariness
- builds close relationships among those who are praying together, horizontally as well as vertically with the Lord[3]

Third, corporate prayer can be a meaningful way to commune with God and others. There are many variations and opportunities for corporate prayer. Participating in your local church, and in Bible studies and cell groups, will give you many opportunities for corporate prayer. It will also build relationships with your brothers and sisters in Christ.

Read Hebrews 10:24–25. How does this apply to corporate prayer in your life?

_____

_____

You may have people at work with whom you can pray. For example, at International Students, our leadership team meets before work on Wednesday mornings to walk around a large lake at a local hotel and pray. As we walk and pray, we talk with God about any kind of need or praise that comes to mind. It's been a wonderful time of corporate prayer. Perhaps you are in a "secular" job, but know other believers where you work. You could meet in the morning before work to pray together, or meet at lunch.

A prayer summit is another way to pray corporately. Dr. Joe Aldrich, former president of Multnomah Bible College and Seminary, began these summits in the late 1980s. He took fifty-two pastors from Salem, Oregon, to the Canon Beach Conference Center on the Oregon coast for four days of prayer and praise. They asked God to show them how to minister to each other as pastors. While together, they spent time praising God, praying, and sharing in community. During the week, the Holy Spirit fell in conviction on this group of pastors, and they were transformed. Individuals stood and publicly confessed to almost every known sin and received cleansing. This summit began a new approach for spiritual leadership: prayer. Today, through this movement and the leadership of Aldrich, the late Terry Dirks, and the Prayer Summit leadership, there have been over six hundred prayer summits for pastors in many different countries.

> *We have every reason to hope*
> *that God is willing, able and ready to*
> *overthrow the status quo in answer*
> *to the united prayers of the saints.*
>
> ———◆◆———
>
> David Bryant

Fourth, you could participate in prayer walks. A prayer walk is just that—walking and praying. People walk around their towns or even drive around and pray for the needs of their cities. You could do this with a group or as an individual through your own neighborhood or other targeted area of your town. Some people have been called to travel overseas and prayer walk through particularly spiritually dark countries, such as Nepal, for God to open spiritual doors.

Another creative way to pray is to simply ask someone to pray with you on the phone or hot mail (instant messaging) on the Internet. Certainly, God wants us to pray directly to Him, and we can do it with others. The Lord told us that we would do greater things after Him (John 5:20; John 14:12). Of course, He meant by the power of the Holy Spirit, but also He could see that technology was coming that would allow us to literally circle the globe in prayer via the Internet or phone lines. God saw great collaborative efforts such as the World Prayer Center in Colorado Springs, which is connected to other locations around the globe for concerted prayer and spiritual warfare.

REVIEW THE DAY

What are some of the patterns of prayer that you exercise in your everyday life? List time alone as well as corporate prayer with individuals or the church.

_____

_____

Through the various possibilities discussed in this section, are there some new means to pray that have come to your attention? Below, plan how to begin new avenues of prayer in your daily life.

_____

_____

Today make a fresh commitment to increase your prayer life. Write a prayer with that commitment below.

_____

_____

What was the most meaningful sentence or Bible verse in this section? Rephrase that particular sentence or verse as a prayer to God.

_____

_____

_____

REVIVAL TRUTHS

- A wide variety of means exist for prayer.
- We need to constantly be aware of the possibilities, and then use some of these means as another way to spend time with God.

KEY VERSE

And in the morning, rising up a great while before day, he went out, and departed into a solitary place, and there prayed. (Mark 1:35)

DAY FOUR

A RIGHT ATTITUDE

How's your heart before God? Heart attitude is everything, for if you are going to pray and desire God to speak to you, then you want to be able to hear His voice. The following are some principles related to a right heart in prayer before God.

First, have the right perspective relative to who God is and who you are. Though God is accessible, we're not just talking to a human friend. When you pray, you enter the holy presence of the eternal God. Can you imagine?

As a believer, you are a high priest. Just as the Old Testament priest went through ritual washings and cleansings before he entered the temple, you approach God's throne with spiritual cleansings of praise, confession, repentance, and a plan to amend any wrongs you've committed. Now, with a clean heart, you're prepared to step into this spiritual relationship with God as the priest stepped into the Holy of Holies.

Second, you need humility of heart so God can speak to you. You can't approach God with pride or a haughty attitude—at least if you expect to have a connection with the God of the universe. If you step humbly into the Lord's presence, then He can speak with you. Read 1 Peter 5:6–7.

> *In revival the town [Northampton] seemed to be full of the presence of God . . . So full of love, joy, and full of distress over sin.*
>
> ———◆———
>
> Jonathan Edwards

Third, be willing to listen. Listening to God is critical. We need to realize how much time we spend talking to God versus listening to Him.

God is always a gentleman; He isn't prone to speak at the same time I am. If I want to hear God, I have to give Him a chance to talk. One way to accomplish this is to combine prayer with fasting. I recommend Dr. Bill Bright's booklet, *7 Basic Steps to Successful Fasting & Prayer.*

What is your heart condition? Take a moment now and ask God to reveal to you where you can grow in this area. Record His response to you.

_____

_____

These three ingredients for prayer—the proper perspective, a humble heart, and a willingness to listen—are clearly seen throughout the Lord's Prayer. As noted previously there is only one case in Scripture where the disciples of Jesus asked for a specific teaching—and it's on the topic of prayer! We can learn a great deal about the ingredients of a heart attitude ready for prayer by studying Jesus' prayer for the disciples (see Matthew 6:9–13).

Jesus began the prayer saying, "Our Father which art in heaven." Through these opening words, He acknowledged the authority and provision of God. He is our Father, to be respected. But He is also our Father whose watch care is constant. If we enter God's presence with a humble heart, we acknowledge God as the Father, the one in charge.

"Hallowed be thy name." The name of God is most holy, and we should revere it. In Hebrew, the word for *name* means "the very essence of the being of the individual." When we use the words, "hallowed be Thy name" it means the very person of God. If you study how people were named in the Old Testament, those names became the character of the individual. The Jewish people understood the reverence for the name of God, and the ultra-conservative Jews today will still not speak the name *Yahweh* out of reverence for the essence of God.

"Thy kingdom come" and "Thy will be done in earth, as it is in heaven." As we recognize our place, His will and desires become our will and desires. Often we approach God with our own agenda looking for Him to bless it, rather than humbly seeking His will. We must listen to God's voice to know His will. And we must seek Him to hear His voice. We submit to the Creator, rather than rebelling as the creation.

"Give us this day our daily bread. And forgive us our debts, as we forgive our debtors." We are to rely on Him for our sustenance, and we are to come to Him with a pure heart. Conviction, confession, and repentance are all important, but so is forgiving others. How can we hold grudges if we don't want God to hold a grudge against us? Because God forgives, we forgive. We must listen to hear God reveal to us our trespasses.

"Lead us not into temptation, but deliver us from evil." We come to Christ with a pure heart, but temptation can carry us away from a pure heart. We ask God to protect us from temptation and to prevent those initial steps toward evil. Satan is always tempting us, but God promises that His children are not tempted above what we're able to withstand (1 Corinthians 10:13). We ask God not to just keep us from temptation, but to keep us from getting into things over our heads, or things not in His plan for us at this time. Even "good" things can take us from "God" things. Only quiet listening and obedience will reveal the steps He wishes us to take.

"For thine is the kingdom, and the power, and the glory." As we pray this, we recognize that God is the owner of all. It is *His* kingdom, it is *His* power, and it is all for *His* glory. We have no ownership, but are blessed because He chooses to include us.

REVIEW THE DAY

The Gospels record two versions of the Lord's prayer, one in Luke 11:2–4 and a longer version in Matthew 6:9–13. Read both of these passages, then write your own insight into the Lord's prayer in your life.

_____

_____

How can the elements of the Lord's prayer help you have a more consistent prayer-like heart attitude? Use the space below to capture your thoughts.

_____

_____

What was the most meaningful sentence or Bible verse in this section? Rephrase that particular sentence or verse as a prayer to God.

_____

_____

_____

What action does God want you to take as a result of today's study? (Perhaps you will want to pray the Lord's prayer often in your daily life.) Meditate, think deeply, and listen to your heart; then write about the action you will take.

_____

_____

REVIVAL TRUTHS

- Heart attitude is critical to hearing God's voice.
- Humility and a willingness to listen are attitudes of a right heart.
- The Lord's prayer models how you are to have a consistent prayer relationship with your Heavenly Father.

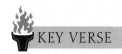

KEY VERSE

After this manner, therefore, pray ye: Our Father which art in heaven, hallowed be thy name. Thy kingdom come. Thy will be done in earth, as it is in heaven. (Matthew 6:9–10)

DAY FIVE

A REMINDER THAT GOD DOES ANSWER

Anyone who has gone to church has heard the pastor say that God does answer prayer; He always answers prayer. A friend of mine shared a string of possible responses from God. Perhaps He says "No," meaning it will never be OK. Or He might say "Grow," meaning He'd like for me to grow more spiritually first. He might ask me to "sow" some seeds before my prayer is answered. Or He might say "Go"—it's a definite yes.

Regardless of which answer comes, He does answer. It may not be the answer I wanted, but it is an answer.

Often we offer our prayers to the Lord with strings attached. Read John 15:7. Under what conditions will God answer our prayers as we desire?

_____

_____

Jesus uses that little word *if* in a powerful way. Abiding in Christ means that we must be as connected to Him as a branch is to the vine of a plant. This is a mandate. In his book, *The Vineyard*, author Wayne Jacobsen wrote, "In the vineyards of this world, branches don't have freedom of choice. They are silent victims of whatever the farmer or his workers decide to be their lot."[4] In God's vineyard, however, we do have a choice. We can choose whether or not to abide.

As the leader of an organization, I see many kinds of people. Two different groups apply in this context. One group in our office often feels that no matter what they suggest, no matter what new thing they attempt in their jobs, it is not well received. There is always a roadblock to stop the idea from developing. Another group almost never has this experience. They make recommendations and changes that are appreciated and implemented. What's the difference? Perhaps the first group doesn't abide in the organization. They are out of sync with the current needs and trends. They don't seem to really understand where we're headed. Consequently, their requests don't fit with the bigger plan. The second group, however, has the pulse of what's needed and where we're going. Their ideas are timely and necessary. They work well with the purposes ahead. They pay attention to the whole picture, not just their individual parts.

I think this same concept is true for prayer. When we are abiding in Christ, He shares with us His desires which then become our desires. Read John 15:14–15. He has called us His friends and shared all that the Father has told Him. When we are connected to Christ, we just know what to pray.

Think about your life. Are you abiding in Christ? How do you know?

_____

_____

What can you do to be more connected to the branch? Make a commitment now to follow your plan.

_____

_____

> *In seasons of distress and grief*
> *My soul has often found relief*
> *And oft escaped the tempter's snare*
> *By thy return, sweet hour of prayer.*
>
> ———◆———
>
> "SWEET HOUR OF PRAYER"/William Walford

It can be extremely difficult for believers to pray and feel as though God does not answer. *World Magazine* noted that media mogul Ted Turner stated he had received Christ as a young man at a Billy Graham Crusade, but moved away from God when his sister died from an illness despite the prayers Ted offered.[5]

Did God answer Ted's prayers? Yes. Did he answer them in the way Ted desired? No. Does God know what is best, in spite of how things appear? Yes. Though we

PRAYER

mourn the loss of loved ones, Jesus assures us that heaven is truly our home, a much better place than earth.

Often believers end up feeling as though God didn't pay attention to them. It's difficult to realize that is a lie from the enemy. God's Word says that He never leaves us or forsakes us (Psalm 37:28). It takes an act of faith to continue walking with the Lord even after disappointment. If we do, however, He will bless us in ways we could never imagine.

Read Psalm 37:3–4. When the author says that God will give us the "desires" of our heart, what does that mean? Will God place the desire, give us what we want, or both?

_____

_____

What are the desires of your heart?

_____

_____

Are they God's desires also? How do you know?

_____

_____

REVIEW THE DAY

Read Psalm 61. Have you ever cried to God "from the ends of the earth" (verse 2)? What was His response?

_____

_____

Is your longing to dwell with God forever? How does your response affect your ability to abide in Christ?

_____

_____

What was the most meaningful sentence or Bible verse in this section? Rephrase that particular sentence or verse as a prayer to God.

_____

_____

_____

What action does God want you to take as a result of today's study? Meditate, think deeply, and listen to your heart; then write about the action you will take.

_____

_____

REVIVAL TRUTHS

- God always answers prayer. Always.
- To best know how to pray, we must abide in Christ.
- We can become discouraged if we believe the lie that says, "God doesn't hear us or answer our prayers."
- God will give us the desires of our heart if we delight in Him.

KEY VERSE

If ye abide in me, and my words abide in you, ye shall ask what ye will, and it shall be done unto you. (John 15:7)

LOOKING AHEAD

Prayer is the channel of communication between the Father and His children. He is always ready to listen, always ready to speak. He always answers. In chapter 6, we'll see how He speaks not just once or twice, but on a continual basis as we are in a continually growing relationship.

6 KNOWING GOD BETTER

In 1904, a young coal miner and Bible college student, Evan Roberts, prayed for God to bend his life, and the Holy Spirit touched him in a profound way. Evan went to his local pastor saying, "I have a message from God for the people." Initially the pastor tried to put him off, but Evan was persistent. Finally the pastor agreed to allow Roberts to speak after the Monday evening prayer meeting. Seventeen people stayed, including the pastor.

His message was simple. "First, turn from any known sin. Second, put doubtful habits out of your life. Third, if you've harmed anyone, go and make it right. Fourth, obey the promptings of the Holy Spirit immediately, and fifth, tell other people about Jesus Christ."

His message wasn't unusual and certainly not unbiblical, and all seventeen people ended up on their knees before God—including the pastor. The pastor asked Evan, "Can you preach tomorrow night?" Evan preached every night for the next week. History records that by the second week you could hardly get through the crowds near the little church. And the results from Evan's prayers and call to a life in Christ? The great pastor James Stewart records, "It was praying that rent the heavens, praying that received direct answers, there and then. The spirit of intercession was so mightily poured out that the whole congregation would take part simultaneously for hours! Strangers were startled to hear the young and unlettered pray with such unction and intelligence as they were swept up to the Throne of

Grace by the Spirit of God. Worship and adoration [were] unbounded. Praise began to mingle with the petitions as answered prayer was demonstrated before their very eyes. Often when unsaved loved ones were the focus of the intercession, they would be compelled to come to the very meeting and be saved!"[1]

These events were the beginning of the Welsh revival, which lasted from 1904–1905. John Peters wrote, in the *Revival World Report*, "The Welsh Revival was immensely successful, with over a hundred thousand conversions, seventy thousand of them reported after a few months."[2]

J.V. Morgan tried to debunk the revival. His research claimed that after five years, of the 100,000 that came to Christ only 80,000 remained in the church. Sounds more like support of the revival than a debunking!

From this spiritual awakening came a time of tremendous social change in Wales—and it started with one man seeking God, Evan Roberts. It requires solitude to hear the still small voice. God is not in the wind or the fire but in the quiet heart that daily listens and obeys.

Our communion with God is not a one-time experience. In a growing relationship, we will meet with Him regularly and hear His voice often. That means planning for and protecting our time with Him. The goal is knowing God better—a worthy goal indeed if He is to wholly use us.

DAY ONE

OUR SPIRITUAL CONNECTION

As director of the 1984 Anchorage Billy Graham Crusade, I visited the Alaskan bush, or remote regions, once or twice. It was amazing to see the nine-foot satellite dishes near various frontier homes. The television dishes would often be sitting on the ground, tilted nearly horizontally because of the angle needed to connect to the satellite signals. To clear the way for the dish signal, the Alaskans would cut a swath of trees away from their TV dishes. If the trees had been left, they would interfere with the signal. Likewise, if anything grew back, or was placed in a satellite's path, it too would interrupt the signal.

In our lives, between our hearts and God's, we need to continually clear away anything that hinders our receptivity to that spiritual communication. To hear God, you have to be an active receptor, a satellite dish tilted toward God. If you want to receive a satellite signal, you don't tilt the dish away from the satellite. The better the focus on the satellite, the stronger the signal. If you clean your heart before God, then you can tilt your heart toward God's throne and, as His words come down, the still small voice can center on your heart. This isn't a one-time event. It's a daily process.

Once you are connected with God, your life as a receptor needs to keep a clear path. Just as the Israelites were given manna for each day, we too must seek God for our daily portion. We do that through many ways:

- Plan time to be alone with Him.
- Seek His face—daily.
- Talk with Him consistently.
- In solitude, stop and listen to Him.
- Cleanse your heart through confessions.
- Surrender your heart in purity.

Once we have done those things, we deal with issues of focus and truth: (1) Focus on who God is; (2) believe in His guidance, that He knows what is best; (3) trust Him; (4) expectantly watch Him work in and through your life; and (5) live in the joy of your relationship.

Imagine eating your only meal on Sunday. Could you possibly eat enough to sustain you for the entire week? Not really, and certainly not with any amount of comfort. Just the thought makes my stomach long for food. And yet, that is how many people attempt to live their life in Christ. One to two hours of church on Sunday, sitting passively in a pew, is all the spiritual food some choose to eat. How sad, when God offers so much more. If only we'll reach out and take it each day. There is more than enough for one day, but not enough for more than one day.

We can't expect remorse without clear and consistent connection with Christ. It's how He always intended our relationship to be.

> *Revival means the outpouring of the Holy Spirit*
> *that inspires the world and the church*
> *with the value of living Christianity.*
>
> David Andrews

Evaluate your own communication with God. How would you rate your receptor connection, with 10 being very close—getting strong signals—and 0 being out of communication?

_____

_____

Take one aspect of your spiritual life and commit to grow in this area—more prayer, more Bible reading, increase in your time of Bible study, fellowship at church, or witnessing. Select one aspect and write down your commitment below.

_____

_____

What is your plan for growth in this area?

_____

_____

What does the Bible say about seeking God? Examine these verses: Deuteronomy 4:29–31, Psalm 27:4, Psalm 40:16, Isaiah 55:6, and Jeremiah 29:13. Write down your discovery from these verses.

_____

_____

To reestablish this spiritual connection requires faith. What does the writer of Hebrews say about the connection between faith and seeking God in Hebrews 11:6? What application can you make to your own life and situation?

_____

_____

REVIEW THE DAY

Each of us must be an active receptor to listen and hear the voice of God. Our first step is to actively seek a connection with God through prayer and a clean heart.

Read Proverbs 8:17. What active step are you making today to seek connection with the Lord of the universe?

_____

_____

As you seek God to make a fresh commitment to reconnect, write a prayer with that commitment below.

_____

_____

What was the most meaningful sentence or Bible verse in this section? Rephrase that particular sentence or verse as a prayer to God.

_____

_____

_____

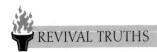

REVIVAL TRUTHS

- God wants us to be active receptors and listen to His voice.
- We must actively seek God's presence in our daily lives.
- Revival requires a constant cleansing of our ability to hear from God.

KEY VERSE

I love them that love me; and those that seek me early shall find me. (Proverbs 8:17)

DAY TWO

KNOWING GOD

A relationship with God can be compared to a marriage. Sometimes a man and woman date for two weeks and then marry. Other couples have known each other since elementary school. Then they complete high school and college before they decide to marry. Even though this second couple knows each other quite well, only through marriage can they enter a world of coexistence and interdependence, one previously unknown. Still, the marriage union will not give one person immediate omniscience about the other.

Because you are seeking a relationship with the Lord of the universe, when you step through the marriage veil of salvation, you receive just a glimpse of what God has to offer. Enjoying any aspect of His gifts hinges on knowing Him and growing in Him. What is amazing is that the knowing and growing never cease. There's great joy as we recognize that the opportunity to grow in our relationship with God is as infinite as the celestial system.

As a young boy in Mississippi, I often went outside during the early evening to help my mom hang clothes on the drying line. Under the starry sky, Mom taught me how to shake out the clothes properly, then hand them to her with clothespins so she could hang them faster. The heat would rise from the clothes in the cold night, warming our hands.

During those nights, as I looked up and saw the sky and stars, the vast nature of the universe would overwhelm me. A couple of autumn evenings in 1957, I watched the Russian spaceship Sputnik cross the horizon during its orbits. Though only 184 pounds, that glittering ball was easy to spot as it swept across the sky. At that time, scientists didn't know as much about the vastness of the universe. We know from God's Word there is an end to creation, perhaps a few to millions of light years away. And still, God is bigger and deeper and *more* than all we can see or imagine.

He created it with the very breath of His words. And the Creator is always greater than the creation. It is the same with our relationship spiritually—there is no limit.

Have you ever heard someone say, "It's not what you know, it's who you know"? In a sense, it's the same in our relationship with God. Not that we try to "use" Him, as if we could without His knowledge, but there are many benefits to a relationship with God.

Let's consider a few of the benefits of knowing God. Examine each benefit and the accompanying verse. What insight do you gain about the benefits of knowing God?

Eternal life (John 17:3)

_____

_____

God in our midst (Isaiah 30:21)

_____

_____

Understanding God's will (Ephesians 5:15–20)

_____

_____

Acceptance of the events in our life (Romans 8:28)

_____

_____

Wisdom of God (1 Corinthians 1:21–23)

_____

_____

REVIEW THE DAY

Is it possible to really know God? Read Ephesians 3:16–19. Here Paul talks about the "size" of God's love. We see from other Scripture that God is infinite—the beginning and the end, the alpha and omega. Psalm 147:5 says that His wisdom is infinite. Given these characteristics, it seems likely that Paul's point was that there is no limit to God's love either. There is no limit to God. Even after an eternity with Him face to face, there will still be more to know.

> *Your love is extravagant*
> *Your friendship intimate. . . .*
> *No greater love have I ever known*
> *You considered me a friend.*
> *Capture my heart again.*
>
> ———
>
> "YOUR LOVE IS EXTRAVAGANT"/Darrell Evans

How are you adding to your relationship with God? List several means below.

_____

_____

What was the most meaningful sentence or Bible verse in this section? Rephrase that particular sentence or verse as a prayer to God.

_____

_____

What action does God want you to take as a result of today's study? (Perhaps He would want you to expand some aspect of your relationship with Him.) Meditate, think deeply, and listen to your heart; then write about the action you will take.

_____

_____

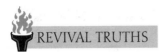

REVIVAL TRUTHS

- God is infinite, and there is always something additional in knowing God.
- There are tangible benefits to a relationship with God.
- The depth of our relationship with God is without confines or limitations.

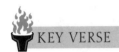

KEY VERSE

May be able to comprehend with all saints what is the breadth, and length, and depth, and height. (Ephesians 3:18)

DAY THREE

SUBMISSION

If I want an intimate, growing, spiritual relationship with God, I will continually die to myself.

When I was forty-six years old, I was the director of counseling and follow-up both nationally and internationally for the Billy Graham Evangelistic Association (BGEA) and the Senior Crusade Director. For a person with the desire to touch the world for Christ through evangelism, this was one of the best jobs one could have; yet I was somewhat uneasy in my spirit.

Six years before that time I had turned to Ouida, my wife, and, relatively new in the director's position, told her: "Honey, I believe that I'm in training for something." Her response was somewhat like that of Sarah when Abraham, then age one hundred, told his wife they would have a child. Ouida said, "How can that be? You're forty years old. You have the best job in evangelism discipleship training and follow-up ministry that anyone in the world could want. You work with someone you trust explicitly, someone whose calling you can follow, someone whose calling is in direct line with the calling God has put on your heart. How could you have any more?"

I don't know if she was disturbed by the possible impact on our family or just shocked that someone my age could be in training for something else!

Later, several opportunities for a change in ministry came my way. The least attractive one in stability was the most attractive in vision. International Students, Inc., a ministry focused on reaching the more than six hundred thousand international students studying in American universities, had gone through a tremendous breaking as an organization. God had accomplished much through the leadership of the board of directors and others, but the job for me would obviously be strenuous. Though many individuals were still supporting ISI, the ministry itself had become weak in management and needed a lot of work. Was I the person God could use? I was inadequate, but I had to trust, to submit to, the authority and adequacy of Christ. Would I leave the strength and stability of the BGEA for an organization still reeling from massive change?

> *Revival begins when*
> *men and women cry out to God.*
>
> Barry Boucher

Think about a decision you faced that required submission to the will of God. How did you respond?

_____

_____

Read Philippians 2:6–11 and Luke 22:39–44. How is Jesus an example to us? How does our sacrifice of submission compare to His?

_____

_____

A tremendous pilgrimage began when I said yes to God and this opportunity to trust Him. Andrew Murray said it so well. "You may not feel it, you may not realize it, but God takes possession if you'll trust Him. . . . Such a life has two sides—on the one side, absolute surrender to work that God wants you to do; on the other side, to let God work what He wants to do."[3]

God answered my prayer to have an opportunity to mold a ministry and I saw myself becoming the president and chief executive officer of International Students. I was thrilled with the possibilities.

But there was much to do. We had a wonderful team of people who remained at ISI—men and women who had done whatever it took to keep the ministry running. Also one of the Board members, Kirk Humphreys, had become the interim CEO for six months, flying from Oklahoma each week for three days in the midst of managing his own business. What a privilege to have such guardians of the vision.

The darkest days were to come as I moved from BGEA, one of the most prayed-for ministries on the face of the globe, to ISI, one that had virtually no prayer covering left. The hours were strenuous; during the first year I would begin at 7 in the morning and work until at least 11 P.M. (sometimes until 3 A.M.). On Saturdays I worked until 6 P.M. and often Sunday afternoons (though I did try to rest on Sundays). I reduced my exercise from daily to about once a week. Meals dropped from three a day to one or two. I had never experienced such a workload except in the middle of a Billy Graham crusade. Working the pace of a one- or two-week crusade for over a year was literally debilitating.

I would have traded those first few years with ISI for almost anything. I felt I had no one to turn to with my concerns and needs. The board had already been through so much. My spiritual mentor couldn't understand my position. My wife didn't need to hear about this all the time. Only Jesus, my Rock, could understand. I would walk Cheyenne Mountain at night for hours at a time crying out to God for His provision.

The economics, the faith in ISI by the donors, the growth of the vision, the restructuring of the ministry, the leadership (certainly myself)—all needed His help, and so many other areas needed His help. It was beyond me to do this job.

We serve a God who is incredibly dependable, and one who carries us when we are obedient far beyond anything we could ever ask or think. But in order for Him to carry me, I had to submit to His will. I had to choose to obey long ago when He first called me into ministry. I again had to choose to leave all that was safe and comfortable after many years with Mr. Graham. I had to daily submit to tough decisions and long hours at ISI.

I didn't always want to submit. I wanted to run sometimes. But as I submitted to where God called me, He remained faithful to complete what He began. Today, He has turned around the ship of ISI from a floundering vessel to one worthy of battle. Christ is being honored.

REVIEW THE DAY

Submission is required in both "big" and "small" areas of life. It's required on an ongoing basis.

Read Ephesians 5:22–6:9. When it comes to submitting, God has an order. Why is that important?

What can happen when we do not submit to God's order?

_____

_____

What causes resistance in you to submit?

_____

_____

What specifically is God calling you to submit to today?

_____

_____

Commit now in prayer that you will submit in every area of life God brings to your attention. Write that prayer.

_____

_____

What was the most meaningful sentence or Bible verse in this section? Rephrase that particular sentence or verse as a prayer to God.

_____

_____

_____

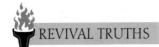 REVIVAL TRUTHS

- Submission is a daily act of obedience to the will of God.
- Submission is not always easy.
- God honors our obedient submission to His will.

KEY VERSE

Saying, "Father, if it is Your will, take this cup away from Me; nevertheless not My will, but Yours, be done." (Luke 22:42 NKJV)

DAY FOUR

PRACTICE THE PRESENCE OF GOD

Born into poverty as Nicholas Herman in French Lorraine in 1611, at age eighteen he accepted Christ as his Savior. A few years later he became a footman—a servant who opened carriage doors and waited on tables, etc. At age fifty-five, he entered a religious community called the Carmelites, located in Paris. Among these bare-footed devotees to Christ, this humble believer and "lay brother" took the name Brother Lawrence. During his twenty-five years in this community, he served mostly in the hospital kitchen.

"He became known, within the community, and later beyond it, for his quiet and serene faith, and for his simple experience of 'practicing the presence of God,'" wrote Frank Lauback in his introduction to Lawrence's classic work, *Practicing His Presence.*

"Eventually Brother Lawrence even received inquiries from people in other parts of France concerning how to have a similar reality in their own daily experience with Christ. Even church leaders sought him out for counsel and help."[4]

Is it possible to be in God's presence twenty-four hours a day? Brother Lawrence believed it was, and his life reflected that belief. Scripture as well indicates that we can remain in His presence. For instance, read Psalm 139:11–12 and John 15:9–10. Let's consider some practical ways to practice His presence.

Scripture gives varying images of the presence of God. At Jesus' baptism, a dove indicated God's presence. In Philippians 4:5 we read that a spirit of gentleness accompanies God's presence. In verse 7 we see that peace indicates God's presence. Today, we know God's presence sometimes only through faith—because He has promised that He will never leave us or forsake us.

How do you recognize God's presence in your life?

A core characteristic of God is *omnipresence*, or being everywhere. Regardless of where we are, in the depths or the heights or in between, God is there. And for the believer, there is greater intimacy with God's presence, for He lives within each who calls Him Lord. In Genesis 28:16 we find Jacob recognizing that the Lord's presence was with him even as a fugitive. What we often lack is the recognition that we are in the presence of God. It is not a warm, fuzzy feeling; it is a fact of who God is. He is in the still small whisper more often than the boom of thunder.

Do you look for the presence of God? Why or why not?

"How do I practice God's presence?" you may ask. First, look for it. Be open to it. Once you begin to recognize it, linger over it. Being in God's presence requires no special skills. It is a relationship and requires communication. We talk to God. We listen to God. He talks to us and listens to us. One way to open the door for recognition is through praise. Psalm 100:4 exhorts us, "Enter into his gates with thanksgiving, and into his courts with praise: be thankful unto him, and bless his name." Practicing the presence of God calls us to recognize His presence, walk by faith that He is there, and communicate with Him always. We are already in His presence; we need to live as such.

> *I have tasted a thrill in fellowship with God which has made anything discordant with God disgusting.*
>
> Frank Laubach

Think about a time when you had a very special guest over to your house, someone you esteemed greatly. How did that affect the way you cleaned your home? How did his presence affect your speech and behavior? Were you more courteous? Did you focus on the guest or yourself? Were you more concerned about how you lived in front of that person? That is not dissimilar from the results of being in God's presence. As we realize that we are in His presence, we become focused on Him.

149

We are concerned about our behavior toward others; we are more cautious about how we live our lives.

I am convinced that when we really believe that we are in God's presence, that He in fact is in us, our hearts and our lives will change from the inside out. We have no choice but to be more like Him.

Have you ever tried to practice the presence of God? What were the results?

_____

_____

How often do you communicate with God during the day? Do you check with Him about all your activities? Why or why not?

_____

_____

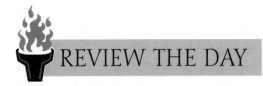

REVIEW THE DAY

As believers we have God living in us—His presence is with us always. It takes a daily recognition of His presence to begin to live in constant communion.

What barriers keep you from recognizing the presence of God? List them, and pray for release from those barriers.

_____

_____

Ask God to teach you how to enter His presence daily. Make a new commitment to daily enter God's presence. Write a prayer with that commitment below.

_____

_____

What was the most meaningful sentence or Bible verse in this section? Rephrase that particular sentence or verse as a prayer to God.

_____

_____

_____

REVIVAL TRUTHS

- God is present with us always.
- We need to recognize His presence on a daily basis.
- As we recognize His presence and commune with Him, our hearts and lives will change.

KEY VERSE

And Jacob awaked out of his sleep, and he said, Surely the Lord is in this place; and I knew it not. (Genesis 28:16)

DAY FIVE

A PLACE
OF REST

The word *rest*, in either Hebrew or Greek, does not mean to sit; it means to trust. Resting in God is an attitude of trust, and this attitude must be fostered daily. At the time of their conversion, people often experience a great sense of peace. This comes from a pure and innocent trust in God. As we continue to grow in our relationship with Christ, it is important to renew that sense of trust in order to rest in God despite the circumstances we face. God is the God of the impossible. What better place to rest?

Early in my ministry with BGEA, I worked as the assistant to Charlie Riggs, the director of counseling and follow-up. Charlie was an example to me of many attributes of God, and resting in God was no exception.

The day before a Billy Graham crusade in Lubbock, Texas, in 1975, I attended a meeting to discuss the need for extra seating. Late in our preparations we realized that that there might be up to 10,000 more people attending the next night than we had originally planned. We didn't have enough chairs. We looked over a diagram of the stadium. Though I was young, I felt my opinion was valuable (could I have been a little prideful?), and didn't mind sharing that I thought it simply could not be done.

Charlie looked up at me and said, "Tom, God needs those chairs for people to hear the Gospel. It not only can be done, but will be done."

Charlie had all the trust in the world that God would accomplish what He needed. We simply had to be obedient. Charlie was a man of action with a heart that rested in the Lord.

The following day, we worked like ants to move every possible kind of chair from the Lubbock churches. By the end of the afternoon, 10,000 plastic, wooden, folding, and aluminum chairs were perfectly placed by volunteers!

What does "resting" imply to you? Is it a positive or negative? Why?

_____

_____

Describe a situation that was stressful, but you knew God called you to rest in Him. Were you obedient? What were the results?

_____

_____

> *Hold me close, let your love surround me;*
> *Bring me near, draw me to your side;*
> *And as I wait,*
> *I'll rise up like the eagle,*
> *And I will soar with You,*
> *Your Spirit leads me on*
> *In the pow'r of Your love.*
>
> —◆—
>
> "THE POWER OF YOUR LOVE"/Geoffrey Bullock

Our culture doesn't promote rest as God desires. We often confuse rest with laziness, or a complete lack of responsibility. I often communicate to the team at ISI that we are to pray like it all depends on God, but work like it all depends on us. That was the example I saw from Charlie Riggs.

Rest is an attitude of the heart. Charlie was one of the hardest working men I knew, but he was able to rest simultaneously. His attitude was that of obedience to God for whatever God asked, not responsibility for the specific outcomes. Because Charlie could separate what God was calling him to do from his human desire to control and manipulate situations for specific outcomes, Charlie could rest. It was God's train; Charlie was just along for the ride.

Read Isaiah 40:28–31. Summarize it below.

_____

_____

What advantages are there to resting in God? How does His stamina compare with our own?

_____

_____

Rest is part of God's plan in creation, both physical and spiritual rest. We are made to sleep every night. Have you ever been around someone who hasn't slept well in a few days? Sleep deprivation is not a pretty sight. It interferes with judgment and reasoning, disrupts emotions, and leaves the body susceptible to sickness. Physical rest is important every day.

Mental rest is important also. There are times when we require a rest from our work so we take a vacation. We may need a rest from any number of activities that we engage in on a regular basis. It's good for us to rest. It's part of God's plan. Even He rested on the seventh day of creation.

Read Matthew 11:28–30. What a blessing to know that spiritually, it is possible to be in a continual state of rest as we trust our Savior. Why is it best to rest in God?

_____

_____

REVIEW THE DAY

Rest is a normal part of our daily life, not something that should happen only occasionally. While we have specific times of physical and emotional rest, we are called to be in continual rest spiritually as we depend on God.

Are you able to rest physically and emotionally on a regular basis? How do you plan for that?

_____

_____

If not, make a plan now to care for your physical and emotional needs.

_____

_____

Why is rest often confused with "laziness"? How does that apply in your life?

_____

_____

Are you able to rest spiritually on a continual basis? Explain your answer.

_____

_____

How can you live in a state of spiritual rest?

_____

_____

What was the most meaningful sentence or Bible verse in this section? Rephrase that particular sentence or verse as a prayer to God.

_____

_____

_____

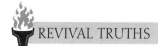

REVIVAL TRUTHS

- Rest is part of God's plan.
- We need physical and emotional rest on a regular basis.
- It is possible to be in a state of continual spiritual rest as we trust in God.

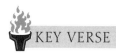

KEY VERSE

Come unto me, all ye that labour and are heavy laden, and I will give you rest. Take my yoke upon you, and learn of me; for I am meek and lowly in heart: and ye shall find rest unto your souls. For my yoke is easy, and my burden is light. (Matthew 11:28–30)

| LOOKING AHEAD |

As we grow in our relationship with Christ, there is a need for continual renewal. Revival in our hearts may begin at a specific point in time, but it never ends there. Daily we are called to renewal through the presence of God's Spirit. As we walk with Him and rest in Him, we open a connection through which He can work to bring revival to others. In the next chapter, we'll see how God bestows gifts for us to use in His kingdom.

7  USING YOUR GIFTS FOR CHRIST

As you watch the news or read a newspaper, it's easy to become discouraged with the state of the world. You feel so small. Is it possible for one person to make a difference? God, in His Word, says "Yes!"

He has endowed us with spiritual gifts to build up the body of believers, to help others know Christ, and also to bring glory to Himself. From the time of creation, we were made to work, and that work was designed to be purposeful in our daily lives. In order to be most effective, God gives each believer work and the gifts needed to complete that work. Many believers fall into a false humility that claims to be "useless," or says, "God can't use me." Some people don't acknowledge they have spiritual gifts at all. The circumstances of life have beaten their reasonable service down to the place where they don't know how or where to serve. This is not pleasing to God. In 2 Timothy 1:6, Timothy is urged not to be shy in using the gift God has given him, but to "stir up the gift," to grow in confidence, and use it.

In order to use our spiritual gifts, it's important for us to recognize them so we can increase our skills and see the service opportunities God has laid before us. When you've established an intimate relationship with God and have started growing in your faith, the natural outflow is to use your talents in the church, the local community, or wherever in the world God directs. Revival calls for all believers to fulfill their role in the body of Christ. And in our service, our lives can remain vibrant for God.

Since most believers have a combination of more than one spiritual gift, I will refer to them in the plural form, as "gifts." In this week's studies, let's discuss spiritual gifts and how to use them in the local body of believers and in your community. While this information has a practical application, the emphasis will continue on "being" in Christ before you attempt to "do" anything. It's critical to continue to grow in your daily walk with the Lord.

DAY ONE

DISCOVER YOUR GIFTS

One of the most difficult people to evaluate is yourself. Certainly you can look in a mirror and see your external features, but it's difficult to see character flaws. It is also a challenge to recognize your gifts. It takes even more work to find a place of service that provides great joy and satisfaction. Some people drift through their entire lives without this knowledge.

Scripture lists a variety of gifts—some say eighteen while others say as many as twenty-seven. While Scripture gives some specific lists, it also implies that other gifts are present as seen through the actions of believers both in the early church and today. Intercession, for example, is not listed on a specific list, but it is evident through the lives of believers who spend countless hours in fruitful prayer for the needs of others. There are a variety of ways to list and categorize spiritual gifts, many of which are variations on the same theme. How does a believer learn about his or her spiritual gifting?

Abundant resources exist today to help the believer on the road to discovery. Books and inventory tests are plentiful. It's important to study several of these and choose one that is grounded in Scripture and helps you determine not just your gifting, but how to best use your gifts. While this is not a comprehensive list, you can find some of these resources listed at the end of this book. I want to mention a few of them here.

C. Peter Wagner's book, *Your Spiritual Gifts Can Help Your Church Grow* (Regal), is an excellent place to begin the study of spiritual gifts. Dr. Wagner provides a list of twenty-seven spiritual gifts, from prophecy to mercy to giving. This is a comprehensive inventory to examine the expression of those gifts in your life, and practical examples of how those gifts can be utilized. Wagner compiled his list primarily from Romans 12:6–8; 1 Corinthians 12:8–10, 28; and Ephesians 4:11. From elsewhere in the New Testament he has added the gifts of celibacy, voluntary poverty, martyrdom, hospitality, and missionary.[1]

Another helpful tool for individual use is Don and Katie Fortune's book *Discover Your God-Given Gifts* (Revell). These authors have separated spiritual gifts into three categories: the manifestation gifts, the ministry gifts, and the motivational gifts. Most helpful in this book is a description of not only gift characteristics, but also the pitfalls of each gift. They give biblical examples of spiritual gifts in action.

A third set of materials available, and one that is good for groups to study, is *Network* (Zondervan). These materials, authored by Bruce Bugbee, Don Cousins, and Bill Hybels, look at spiritual gifts from three perspectives: determining where your passions lie, seeing what skills or spiritual gifts God has given, and determining your personal style for how to best put those passions and skills to work. These materials focus on the interdependence of believers to confirm our gifts and how to use those gifts.

> *Lord, I offer my life to You,*
> *Everything I've been through,*
> *Use it for Your glory.*
>
> ———◆———
>
> "I OFFER MY LIFE"/Claire Cloninger and Don Moen

As you can see just by this short description, there is a lot to read and study in the area of discovering your spiritual gifts. If you have not done so, I recommend that you obtain at least one of these resources and study more in depth the topic of spiritual gifts. It's important, however, not to make it too complicated. Beginning with these simple questions will help set you on the right course.

What are the desires of your heart?

_____

_____

Do others around you affirm this desire in you as something you can do well? Who has affirmed you, and in what way?

_____

_____

In what areas of service do you find joy? In what areas of service have you clearly known you were right where God called you to be?

_____

_____

The answers to these questions are a good place to begin to discover your spiritual gifts.

As you begin to understand your gifting, I have one huge caution: If people ask you to do things that are outside your area of gifting, don't hesitate to say, "No, thank you." Too often with other believers we hesitate to say no, and the result is working outside of our abilities and gifts, perhaps with limited joy or productivity.

Our daughter, Cara, is a physician. As she considered her gifts and how to use them to serve in her church, she felt drawn to the high school age group. Yet her church wanted her to work in Sunday school with younger children. This misplacement happens frequently in the body of Christ; so many people are not functioning where God has called them that there appears to be a shortage of workers. Churches are forced to continue the trend of misplacement to meet felt needs. Yet, if we all functioned according to our gifts, there would likely be just enough help to go around. It's important to discover your spiritual heart, and, when you find it, don't work in the wrong area—no matter how much you are pressured.

Keep in mind that your strengths and abilities are from God. As you discover your passion and gifting, commit these into God's hands and ask Him to show you how and where to use them. If you are resting in His guidance, then God will put the tapestry of your life together.

What does the Bible tell us about this process of receiving and using our spiritual gifts? Read 1 Corinthians 12:1, 11; 1 Peter 4:10.

_____

_____

REVIEW THE DAY

As you understand your spiritual gifts, they can have a far-reaching impact on the world around you—in your local body of believers and your community at large. The first step is discovery.

USING YOUR GIFTS FOR CHRIST

List a key spiritual gift you have either newly discovered or one that has been confirmed through this process. Why is it key for your life?

_____

_____

Read 2 Timothy 1:6. How can you apply this in your life?

_____

_____

Today make a new commitment for God to use your spiritual gift. Write a prayer with that commitment below.

_____

_____

What was the most meaningful sentence or Bible verse in this section? Rephrase that particular sentence or verse as a prayer to God.

_____

_____

_____

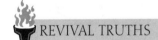 REVIVAL TRUTHS

- God calls us to discover the spiritual gifts He has given to us.
- Our spiritual gifts, when exercised for Christ, will give you great joy and fulfillment.
- Others can help you identify your spiritual gift. Remember there is safety in a multitude of counselors.

 KEY VERSE

Therefore I remind you to stir up the gift of God which is in you through the laying on of my hands. (2 Timothy 1:6 NKJV)

DAY TWO

DEVELOPING YOUR SPIRITUAL GIFTS

OK, so now that you've become familiar with the wonderful spiritual gifts God has given you, what's next? Sometimes I wish God would just "zap" me into the finished product He intended for me to be, but He never seems to work that way. Our God is a God of order, and He likes to take us through the process of becoming a finished product. It is the same with the spiritual gifts He bestows upon us. Let's look at how we can take the knowledge of our gifts and learn to develop what we have discovered. This involves six steps: (1) present your newly discovered gifts, (2) plan how to develop your gifts, (3) know the pitfalls of your gifts, (4) personalize your gifts by studying their use in Scripture, (5) pray about your gifts, and (6) practice using your gifts.

> *All the worry and fret of God's children*
> *would end if their eyes were opened to see the*
> *greatness of the treasure hid in their hearts. . . .*
> *You carry God in your heart!*
>
> ———◆———
>
> Watchman Nee

A good first step is to present your newly discovered gifts. Depending upon your church structure and lifestyle, you might share it with your pastor, a spiritual mentor, your accountability partner, or fellowship group. It is important to tell others, however. By telling what God is teaching us, we reinforce that information and it helps us to grow. Sharing the information with your spouse is important, but also sharing it within the body of believers will provide a natural means of accountability. Pray about whom God would have you first discuss your spiritual gifts.

Write that information below and make definite plans to follow through.

_____

_____

Read Romans 10:10, James 5:16, and 1 John 1:9. Why is confession to others important?

_____

_____

In telling others about your spiritual gifts, include an open door for accountability; it's a vital part of the body of Christ. *Others can help you in following a plan for how to develop your gifts.* As we continue in this section, we'll discuss ways to help you grow in using your spiritual gifts. Use those, and any other ideas you have, in your plan. Consider Proverbs 16:9 as you develop your plan.

Telling others also means you can have valuable insight when you function outside of your area of gifting. For example, let's say you have the gift of leadership but not the gift of mercy. You are asked to commit every Saturday to hospital visitation. Is that the best way to use your time, given your gifts? Probably not. But sometimes it takes an outsider's perspective to see that—if we're willing to listen.

Just a word about making decisions for where to serve. As believers, we have a general calling in Christ and a specific calling through our gifts. We are all called to tell others about Christ (general call), but not all of us have Billy Graham's gift of evangelism (specific). We never have an excuse to not help someone because we don't have the gift of "helps," or to not be kind to someone because we aren't merciful. Our gifting allows us to see where we can focus our time to serve; it doesn't give us an excuse to avoid something we'd rather not do.

Take a moment now and jot down a basic plan for growing in your gifts. Be specific. Then share that plan with someone who can help you be accountable.

_____

_____

While you don't want to become burdened with excessive information, it's important to take time to read materials written on spiritual gifts, such as some of those listed earlier in this chapter. *A key element is knowing the pitfalls of your gifts.* Fortune's *Discover Your God-Given Gifts* is an excellent resource for spotting the potential pitfalls of spiritual gifts. Any strength, taken to its extreme, will become a liability. For instance, the person with the gift of exhortation runs the risk of being outspoken and opinionated. Take time to study the potential pitfalls associated with your gift. Ask God to convict you in those areas and help you to change. None of us are perfect. Read James 1:5.

What are the major pitfalls associated with your spiritual gifts?

_____

_____

Pray now and ask God to help you see behaviors that need to be changed. Record those behaviors here.

_____

_____

Be sure to personalize spiritual gifts, recognizing them in biblical characters. Many believers forget that the individuals in Scripture were real people who had different gifts and callings. Study biblical characters to understand their strengths and weaknesses, and to see how God used particular spiritual gifts. An excellent resource showing biblical examples of gifts in action would be the Fortunes' book, *Discover Your God-Given Gifts.* You could also do a character study. Pick a character in Scripture with whom you identify and analyze the person according to spiritual gift inventories. It may take some time, and you won't always find one with "your gifts" right away, but it's a rich exercise worth the effort.

List a biblical character with whom you identify. Why do you identify with this character?

_____

_____

What spiritual gifts seem present in this person's life? How do you see the strengths and the pitfalls of those gifts?

_____

_____

We've talked a great deal about prayer throughout this book. It is foundational. Next, pray about your spiritual gifts. Pray that God would help you keep focused on using them for His glory and not your personal gain. Pray about the pitfalls. Pray about where God would have you serve in using those gifts.

Finally, practice using your gifts. This can sometimes be the most difficult and yet most fruitful way to grow in using our spiritual gifts. Basically, you can't develop your gifts until you use them. The rub lies in that while we are learning, we fail. God is gracious to let us fail and teaches us through that process, but we humans usually avoid practice until we're perfect. (Or we foolishly think we are!) This is where planning, under the direction of the Holy Spirit, is so helpful. Just as we exercise our physical muscles and they grow to allow us to do more-challenging activity, if we exercise our spiritual gifts we'll also grow in their use.

We'll often fail as we try. But if we continue to pray, to seek God's desire, to step out in faith where God directs, we'll fail less and see fruit more. Don't forget that all things work together for God's good (see Romans 8:28). God uses us in His plan, but the fruit rests with Him.

With regard to your spiritual gifts, take a moment now and pray. What is God saying to you?

List some areas where you can begin to exercise your spiritual gifts. Are these areas included in your plan to grow? If not, add them.

REVIEW THE DAY

What was the most meaningful sentence or Bible verse in this section? Rephrase that particular sentence or verse as a prayer to God.

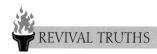
REVIVAL TRUTHS

- After we discover our spiritual gifts, it's important to develop them for use.
- Spiritual gifts are for God's glory, not our personal gain.
- To grow in our spiritual gifts, we must practice using them.

KEY VERSE

If any of you lack wisdom, let him ask of God, that giveth to all men liberally, and upbraideth not; and it shall be given him. (James 1:5)

DAY THREE

SERVING IN YOUR CHURCH

As a young pastor in Mississippi, I tried to sing with the youth choir. I faithfully attended practice and sang with all my heart. I loved singing praises to God. One day, a member of the choir pulled me aside and said, "Pastor, we need to practice the special." Then he continued, most honestly I would add, "And your singing is so bad that we can't get it right." In other words, please be quiet. I heard the message, immediately gave up my position in the choir, and have never tried to enter that arena again. It's outside of my particular range of talents. Music brings me fulfillment, but I really have no ability in this area. My attempt to serve in an area where I was not gifted was a hindrance to others who were serving where God had called them.

It's important for you to consider the body of believers with whom you worship. How do your gifts match with the needs of your local church? For the purposes of this discussion, let's assume that the church you attend is grounded in Scripture and reflects Christ.

Consider Paul's words in 1 Corinthians 12:12–26. Take a moment and read those verses now. How did God organize the body of Christ?

_____

_____

Why is it important for each believer to do his part?

_____

_____

What happens if people try to serve outside of their calling?

_____

_____

Think about your own church. What are the needs you hear about most frequently? List those here.

_____

_____

How do those needs match with your gifts?

_____

_____

> *I have a destiny in that city on a hill.*
> *I have a destiny and it's not an empty wish.*
> *For I know I was born for such a time as this.*
>
> —◆—
>
> "I HAVE A DESTINY"/Mark Altrogge

Have you considered less "publicized" needs, such as giving rides to those without a vehicle, or cleaning up after a special event? Other less-known needs might include things your church hasn't done in the past, but that you might be able to coordinate and/or provide. For example, you might be able to fix cars. Most churches have plenty of single women or elderly people who would appreciate someone's ability to help with minor car repair. The bottom line is, don't limit yourself or your church. If you're good at doing it, someone probably needs it!

List any other areas in your church where you can serve according to your gifts.

_____

_____

A caution about serving within the body of believers: Sometimes it's easy to notice the gifts and talents of others and begin to feel as though our gifts are "less important." This is especially true if we compare the more public gifts of teaching and preaching to the gift of helps—which often means behind-the-scenes work. We have been conditioned to see things this way. What is most important is not who has the most valuable gift, because in God's eyes they are all equally valuable, but just have a different place in the body. (Review 1 Corinthians 12:18–27.) It's most important that we keep our eyes focused on Christ and serve motivated by obedience to Him and Him alone.

REVIEW THE DAY

Keep in mind that God is the one who meets the needs of others. While He uses us in the process, He will be the ultimate provider. As needs arise in your church, be sure that you are called to say yes. Being distracted by good things can prevent you from "God" things.

How can you plan to serve more at your church according to your gifts?

_____

_____

What was the most meaningful sentence or Bible verse in this section? Rephrase that particular sentence or verse as a prayer to God.

_____

_____

_____

What action does God want you to take as a result of today's study? Meditate, think deeply, and listen to your heart; then write about the action you will take.

_____

_____

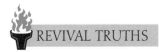

REVIVAL TRUTHS

- It's important to know the needs of your church.
- Match those needs with your spiritual gifts to determine your place of service.
- Consider both the publicized needs and those less publicized as areas of service.
- Be willing to start an area of service if you see a need that isn't being met.

KEY VERSE

But now hath God set the members every one of them in the body, as it hath pleased him. (1 Corinthians 12:18)

DAY FOUR

SERVE YOUR COMMUNITY

Though we often begin serving in our local church, your gifts may be used beyond those four walls. It's important to remember that we are gifted to build up the body of believers for a purpose—"For the perfecting of the saints, for the work of the ministry" (Ephesians 4:12). We need to remember that the non-believers outside our church walls are counting on those works of service as a demonstration of God's love. But because of perceived needs in the church, the community is often neglected. I say "perceived" because there are times when a particular program or plan creates work without building up the body. In this section I will encourage you to become involved in your community.

> *Preach the Gospel at all times,*
> *and, if necessary, use words.*
>
> ———
>
> St. Francis of Assisi

In Scripture, we see that Jesus was involved in His community. He attended social events, such as weddings, and participated in the religious ceremonies of his day. We also see that Jesus offered a social aspect to the Gospel.

Read Matthew 25:31–46. Summarize Jesus' message about caring for others.

_____

_____

Does Jesus specify whether those we help are part of the body of Christ? What difference does it make?

_____

_____

Though food and shelter are specific, they may also serve as an example to us that God calls us to be involved with others. There are other ways to serve in your community besides a homeless shelter or food bank. But how do you find out where you can serve? You might begin by reading your local newspaper. Consider civic groups and clubs that have objectives that match your goal to serve.

Look in your newspaper. What kinds of stories grab your attention?

_____

_____

Do any of these stories give you ideas of how you might get involved and serve? Which ones?

_____

_____

Some believers have separated themselves from society. Jesus does not give us that example. He fully participated in social and cultural events, in fact. His first public miracle (as recorded in John) was performed at a wedding. Jesus attended funerals and feasts. He was part of the society in which He lived. He even worked at a "secular" job as a carpenter before beginning full-time ministry.

Don't be afraid to participate in your community. God is counting on you to touch the lives of those who don't know Him. That's impossible if you don't move beyond the four walls of your church. You are Jesus with skin, and may be the only Jesus some people ever see. Let Him serve through you.

REVIEW THE DAY

Read John 2:1–11 and Luke 22:7–12. What were the circumstances?

_____

_____

In what social/community activities do you participate?

_____

_____

List others that interest you. Make a plan to increase your involvement in the community.

_____

_____

What was the most meaningful sentence or Bible verse in this section? Rephrase that particular sentence or verse as a prayer to God.

_____

_____

_____

REVIVAL TRUTHS

- Church is not the only place we can serve.
- God calls us to be involved in our communities.
- Non-believers in the community can see God's love in action through us.

KEY VERSE

For I was an hungred, and ye gave me meat: I was thirsty, and ye gave me drink: I was a stranger, and ye took me in: naked, and ye clothed me: I was sick, and ye visited me: I was in prison, and ye came unto me. (Matthew 25:35-36)

DAY FIVE

SACRED OR
SECULAR WALK

The observant editor of *Discipleship Journal*, Sue Kline, once wrote a column about her visit to a snowboard shop. The attitude of one young employee there, complete with body piercings and tattoos, impressed her. The snowboard shop guy treated people with cheerfulness and respect, and loved helping his customers—all attitudes of Christ. The author revealed that on the same day she visited the snowboard shop, she struggled to be like Christ in her "sacred" work. She was impatient, complaining, and gossipy . . . with the attitude of someone working in full-time ministry. Her question to the reader was "Which work was secular and which was sacred?"[2]

In the American church, Christians typically place their work into two distinct categories. One is the secular; the other is the sacred. Traditionally, sacred work is defined as within a church or a parachurch organization, performing full-time Christian work as both their ministry and livelihood; or in the case of a missionary, serving with little or no pay. Thus we have Christian musicians, Christian booksellers, and even Christian Internet sites, operated, of course, by Christian entrepreneurs. In contrast, secular work is seen as anything outside of a full-time ministry. But are any of these former jobs better just because they have a "Christian" label? What makes one Christian and the other not?

Where I live, in Colorado Springs, more than one hundred Christian ministry organizations operate. It's easy to bump into other ministry folks, and the community is well aware of the vast number of "Christian workers." What can be distressing, however, is that sometimes there is no difference between the attitudes of the believers and those of the non-believers. Or even worse, those proclaiming Christ through full-time service behave *less* like Christ than unbelievers do. For example, one local pastor admonished his church about their behavior in restaurants after the Sunday morning service. Several restaurant workers disliked working on Sundays because the "church people" were so cheap. They lingered at tables for hours, the pastor explained, keeping the tables from other hungry customers, and then leaving a meager tip. That's hardly an attitude of Christ.

As you discover and develop your spiritual gifts, you may feel a call into full-time service with a church or other Christian agency. If that's from God, that's wonderful. Be obedient. Go where He leads. But you may also feel confirmation to stay in your job outside the Christian arena, or even move from a job with a Christian agency to one with a secular organization. That's good too.

Paul exhorted the church, "And whatsoever ye do, do it heartily, as to the Lord, and not unto men" (Colossians 3:23). We were created for work. In Genesis 2:15, we see the first work God commissioned was farming—tending the garden. This would not be considered a "Christian" job today—unless you worked as a church groundskeeper! Jesus has called His followers to be salt and light to the world (see Matthew 5:13–16), a clear indication that we should bring the flavor of God to those who don't know Him.

> *I surrender all,*
> *I surrender all,*
> *All to Thee, my blessed Savior,*
> *I surrender all.*
>
> —◆—
>
> "I SURRENDER ALL"/Judson W. VandeVenter

What is most important, what makes work secular or sacred, is not the work itself, but the attitude of the heart. How do you treat others? What kind of attitude and work ethic do you carry? Don't get caught believing that one calling is higher than another. Get caught exemplifying the fruits of the Spirit as you use the gifts of the Spirit wherever God has placed you.

Read Galatians 5:22–26. What are the fruits of the Spirit?

_____

_____

How do those compare with the sins listed ("works of the flesh") in Galatians 5:19–21?

_____

_____

How could Galatians 5:26 relate to comparing secular or sacred work?

_____

_____

Someone serving in a Christian ministry, when God has not called him or her there, is not doing sacred work but rather is working in the flesh. It is a temptation to base our worth on our work, and so it sometimes feels more "godly" to be in Christian service. This is a lie from the enemy. God will use your spiritual gifts perfectly in the place to which He has called you. Revival depends on believers touching the lives of unbelievers. That's impossible if we don't even know any. Listen to His voice and obey. Wherever God is—that's holy and sacred work.

REVIEW THE DAY

Do you work in a "secular" or "sacred" job? Explain your answer.

_____

_____

Are you tempted to value yourself based on your work? Why is this not according to Scripture? Read 2 Corinthians 3:4–5.

_____

_____

How do you use your spiritual gifts in your daily work?

_____

_____

How can you use them more?

_____

_____

What was the most meaningful sentence or Bible verse in this section? Rephrase that particular sentence or verse as a prayer to God.

_____

_____

REVIVAL TRUTHS

- Our work is secular or sacred because of our attitude, not our job.
- The fruits of the Spirit are a measuring tool for the "sacredness" of our work.
- We are to work where God calls us, using our spiritual gifts to glorify Him.
- Our value comes from God, not our work.

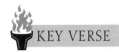

KEY VERSE

Let your light so shine before men, that they may see your good works, and glorify your Father which is in heaven. (Matthew 5:16)

LOOKING AHEAD

Functioning within the spiritual gifts God has given you is a vital component for revival in our lives. The body will be sick and ineffective unless we're all doing our part. In chapter 8, we'll see how using our gifts gives the opportunity for evangelism with great results.

8 THE PRACTICAL RESULTS OF EVANGELISM

The word *evangelism* originated from the Greek word *euangelion*, which is translated "the Gospel." Within the structure of this word *euangelion* is the word *evangel*, which means "good news." Among the early English, it was called "God's Spell." It was said that the good news of God will put "God's spell" on the person who would receive it. This is good news—God's nature, purpose, power, and love incorporated in the human vessel.[1]

Followers of God desire to know Him and to make Him known—to share the good news of spiritual rebirth through Jesus Christ. In marriage we reproduce offspring; similarly, as Christians we are called to spiritually reproduce. The faith by which we live is transferable from one person to another. That's evangelism.

Often people say about me, "Tom's heart is revival." My heart is really evangelism, but the heartbeat to get it there is revival. For mass numbers to make commitments to a relationship with God, it will take a renewed and revived church. Each person's fire must be rekindled. That leads to explosive evangelism—through the cleansing of the church and the unhindered flow of the Holy Spirit. The goal in revival is to see evangelism explode as it has historically during and after other great awakenings.

Evangelism is what revival is all about. Many think that revival is evangelism. No; revival is preparing the church for evangelism. It's the process for preparing the church for the reproduction God intends.

Will you be one to tell others? Do you want to be?

DAY ONE

A BURDEN FOR OTHERS

At the time of our salvation, as we begin our walk with Christ, most of us are burdened only for ourselves. We focus on our relationship with God. We've read about it and heard about it and people from history have talked about it. And so, we want it. Our burden is for our own soul.

Then, as we understand the preciousness of our relationship with Christ and the wonder of daily grace and mercy, we look around at our loved ones and say, "They need to know Jesus." Soon we begin to notice those outside our family and relatives as well, those we know well and those we know little or not at all. We see emptiness. We realize that without Christ all that waits is an eternity in hell. We conclude, rightly, "Everyone should have a chance to know Him."

How do you develop this passion for others? First, recognize it's not a human passion. It's an eternal passion that comes from the heart of God. In the natural flesh, our only burden is for self, but, as we are renewed, we walk in an intimate relationship with Jesus. He begins to show us others.

The following song, entitled "Lead Me to Some Soul Today," reflected the heart of D. L. Moody, who witnessed to someone every day. There are stories of Moody getting out of bed at 11 P.M. telling his wife, "I forgot to witness today." He went onto the street and buttonholed the first person he encountered, who often responded, "Who . . . oh, Dr. Moody?" The people in his neighborhood knew Moody and his love for the souls of others. On a consistent basis, Moody led people to a personal relationship with Jesus Christ.[2]

> *Lord lead me to some soul today.*
> *O teach me, Lord, just what to say;*
> *Friends of mine are lost in sin*
> *and cannot find their way.*
> *Few there are who seem to care*
> *and few there are who pray;*
> *Melt my heart and fill my life.*
> *Give me one soul today.*
>
> ————————
>
> "LEAD ME TO SOME SOUL TODAY"/Will H. Houghton

One day, after singing "Lead Me to Some Soul Today," I told God, "Here I am in seminary learning how to tell others about you, and I don't tell people about you every day. Lord, I'm going to make a pact with you. If you will bring somebody into my path every day for two weeks, I'll witness to them." It happened through God—not an engineered deal forced in my flesh. Each day He brought someone whom I could tell about Jesus Christ.

At the end of those two weeks, I said to the Father, "Lord, this has been wonderful and it has not been embarrassing. There has not been pressure on me or on these people. They've just been there and ready to hear. It's been absolutely incredible." Then, in prayer, I asked, "Daddy, where have these people been before?"

God spoke to my heart and said, "Tom, they've been there all along. Where have you been?"

I was so busy and caught up in being Tom that I never saw them. Business with my family, my full-time job, my church on the weekends, and my full-time student work at seminary kept me walking past people who were separated from God. I was studying to tell others the truth of Jesus and His salvation, but was so task-oriented I ignored the privilege of "relationship proclamation"—telling those whom I meet, including those with whom I have only a casual relationship, about God's love through Christ. I'm not suggesting that you witness to every person you meet, but is your heart right to hear God when He directs you toward someone in your path?

Have you ever felt the urge to share with someone? How did you respond? Were you obedient?

_____

_____

Is your heart in a place to hear from God on a moment-by-moment basis? How can you ready yourself to hear and obey?

_____

_____

Maybe you've never shared Christ's story with someone before. Maybe you don't have a burden for others. You are not alone. God will grow that desire as you ask Him to do so. Here are some tips for you to begin to gain this burden for souls. *First, study the Word of God to see His heart for evangelism.* Read 2 Corinthians 6:2 and look up other Scriptures on the subject. *Second, pray and ask God to show you the needs of the people around you.* As we see others through God's eyes, their need for Him becomes clear. *Third, remember that you are sharing the most important aspect of your life.* It's interesting how people will behave like screaming maniacs during a football game and yet be embarrassed to share about the God of the universe. Keep it in an eternal perspective. Are you really embarrassed of God? *Fourth, remember you and I are called to be "witnesses."* We are only expected to share what we have seen God do in our own lives. We are not required to know every answer to every question. Relax. You know the miracles God has performed in your life.

Three ways to prepare for sharing your faith are: (1) take a class on witnessing or apologetics, or even an overview of the Bible to help you gain confidence in sharing with others; (2) find a tool that will help you share your faith. (On the resource page, you'll see a booklet entitled *Knowing God Personally*; it provides a simple means to present Christ.); and (3) if you have plans to share with someone, ask others to pray for you during that time.

God promises that He will finish what He has begun (Philippians 1:6). While we often feel pressure to get "results," remember that although you may present the Gospel, only God can save.

REVIEW THE DAY

Review the tips for increasing your burden for the lost and ways to prepare to share your faith. What stands out as a need in your own life to increase your burden for the lost? Write some concrete plans in the blanks that follow.

_____

_____

Our heavenly Father is like the shepherd who searches diligently for the lost sheep. We can help guide the lost who are near us. Turn to Matthew 18:12–14. What insight do you gain about the diligent search of God for the lost? Write your thoughts below.

_____

_____

Think for a moment about someone in your life who doesn't have a personal relationship with Jesus. How can you be Jesus to that person? Write the person's name below and begin to pray daily for them. Ask God for openings to talk about spiritual matters with this person.

_____

_____

What was the most meaningful sentence or Bible verse in this section? Rephrase that particular sentence or verse as a prayer to God.

_____

_____

_____

REVIVAL TRUTHS

- A pure heart helps us see others through God's eyes.
- There are ways to increase our burden to share.
- It's important that we are not so busy doing our own thing that we miss God's direction to share with others around us.

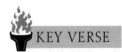

KEY VERSE

For the Son of man is come to save that which was lost. (Matthew 18:11)

DAY TWO

EVANGELISM AS AN INDICATION OF REVIVAL

The evangelist Charles Finney noted seven indicators of a coming revival.[3] Many of these are components that lead us to evangelism. Let's examine each of these indicators since their presence may indicate an awakening. Are these signs operative in your life?

1. Revival comes when the sovereignty of God indicates a revival is at hand. Do you sense a movement of the Spirit of God in your own life? Is your spirit drawing to God's Spirit? Is there a desire to be intimate with Jesus Christ? Write your response.

_____

_____

2. Revival comes when wickedness grieves and humbles Christians. Does the wickedness of the world distress you as a follower of Christ? When you read the newspaper or look at television or the Internet, does this information grieve you? Have you reached a point as you pray about this wickedness that you are grieved about your own wickedness? Your own pet sins? Your own lack of faith or of love? Your own lack of obedience to God? Write your response.

_____

_____

3. Revival comes when followers of Christ pray for revival. Do you pray for God to awaken His church in this country? Do you pray that an awakened church will reach out and touch the souls of men and women spiritually and socially? Write your response.

4. Revival comes when the attention of ministers is especially directed toward revival. Have you noticed your pastor is preaching and teaching more and more about the need for an awakened nation? An awakened church? As a lay minister of the Gospel, are you praying for and interested in an awakened heart? An awakened denomination? Write your response.

5. Revival comes when Christians begin to confess their sins to one another. Is this indicator operative in your life? Are you conscious of sin in your life? Do you have a desire to confess your sins to God and those you offend? Do you have an accountability partner or group? Write your response.

6. Revival comes when followers of Christ are willing to make the sacrifices necessary to carry on the movement God has started, regardless of the personal cost. Are you at a point where you see that nothing is more important in your family, your city, your state, this nation, or the world, than a relationship with God? Are you willing to sacrifice, if God should ask? Are you willing to say to God, "God, I love You and I trust You so much. You are my Daddy. I will give You everything I've got, and You can use it any way that You want." Are you willing? Write your response.

Bill Bright is a good example of someone willing to sacrifice for his relationship with Jesus. As a wealthy young businessman with international concerns, Bill listened when God spoke to him and his wife, Vonette. They got on their knees and turned everything over to God. As a young man, he had promised his wife an expensive home in Beverly Hills, yet they turned it over to God and signed a contract to give everything to God. They presented their lives as a living sacrifice to God, and the Lord has blessed in a fabulous way through the ministry of Campus Crusade for Christ. God is not your employer. He's your Lord. Are you willing to be His slave? Sometimes we think sacrifice is a big deal.

Read Paul's words in Romans 12:1. What is the expectation for sacrifice on our part?

_____

_____

7. Revival comes when ministers and laity are willing for God to promote spiritual awakening by whatever instrument He pleases. For example, are you willing for God to use you to promote this movement? Will you allow God to use your children, or do you have plans for their future that wouldn't permit them to follow God's call? The Lord does not call everyone into full-time vocational ministry, but He does call all into full-time service for Him. Write your response.

_____

_____

> *I love you, Lord,*
> *And I lift my voice*
> *To worship You,*
> *O my soul, rejoice.*
>
> ———◆———
>
> "I LOVE YOU LORD"/Laurie Klein

REVIEW THE DAY

In 2 Corinthians 2:14–15, the Scriptures describe how we are "the fragrance of Christ" to draw others who are perishing to the knowledge of Christ. Read this passage, then reflect on your life. How are you a fragrance of Christ? What steps can you take to ensure your aroma is pleasing? Write some action steps below.

_____

_____

THE PRACTICAL RESULTS OF EVANGELISM

Read Matthew 9:35–38. Consider the ministry of Jesus and His admonition that His disciples pray for the lost. What insight do you gain about your own life and the need for prayer for the lost? Write what you learn below.

_____

_____

What type of sacrifices are you making or are willing to make for your relationship with Christ to reach a lost and dying world? Are you willing to be willing? If so, then write a prayer of commitment below.

_____

_____

What was the most meaningful sentence or Bible verse in this section? Rephrase that particular sentence or verse as a prayer to God.

_____

_____

_____

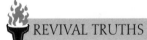

REVIVAL TRUTHS

- The seven indicators of a coming revival are: (1) God's sovereign moving in the church, (2) grief and humility over wickedness, (3) prayers for revival, (4) pastors focusing on revival, (5) Christians beginning to confess sins to each other, (6) Christians willing to sacrifice, and (7) pastors and laity willing for God to promote spiritual awakening by whatever instrument He pleases.
- God is our Lord, and He calls on us to present our lives to Him as living sacrifices, even as Bill and Vonette Bright did.

KEY VERSE

For we are unto God a sweet savour of Christ, in them that are saved, and in them that perish. (2 Corinthians 2:15)

DAY THREE

A PREPARED
HEART

Many years ago at the Forest Home Conference Center in California's San Bernardino Mountains, a young Billy Graham knelt down by a stump with his Bible. He knew that intellect alone couldn't answer his questions about the authority of Scripture. He needed to have faith in his heart that God's Word was true. Billy prayed, "Oh, God; I cannot prove certain things. I cannot answer some of the questions . . . people are raising, but I accept this Book by faith as the Word of God."[4] He was making a commitment to go proclaim God's Word faithfully, and knew that in order to do that his heart had to be prepared by faith.

A daily openness for evangelism comes first with a daily openness to God. Each of us must be able to pray, "God, I'm open to You today. I want to be obedient to whatever You put before me." If our attitude isn't right, we can't be available for Him to work through us. We need to remember that no matter what we have planned, our day—each day—belongs to God.

> ### *Revival is . . .*
> *God's quickening visitation of His people,*
> *touching their hearts and*
> *deepening the work of grace in their lives.*
>
> —◆—
>
> J. I. Packer

Sometimes I get so caught up in the "work" of God that my heart attitude is one of production rather than people. I feel busy as a CEO of an evangelistic organization, and I travel frequently. When I get on an airplane, it's often the first time I've had alone in quite a while. My flesh says, "Oh, God, don't let anybody sit by me who will take my time." I know that's not an open attitude, but sometimes I really feel that way. I'm sure I can trust God completely to know my needs and care for me, but my flesh is selfish. He knows when I need time to remain alone, and He knows when I need to share His Word with others.

Read Matthew 14:1–14. What are the circumstances in verses 1–12? Why did Jesus, in verse 13, feel the need to go off by Himself?

_____

_____

In spite of His feelings, what was Jesus' response to the crowd?

_____

_____

Why was that the "right" thing for Jesus to do? (See John 14:31 for a hint.)

_____

_____

Perhaps the key to a prepared heart is in how you start your day. We see the example of Christ making time in the early morning to be alone to pray; read Mark 1:35. What is your attitude in starting your day? Do you get a jump start on your to-do list, or do you first consult the Master of the universe about *His* plans for you? Are you willing to get up in the morning and say to Father God, "I'm your slave. I want to have an intimate relationship with You today. I want to sense Your presence all day long. I know I have plans, but I want to be available for Your plans. I want You to guide me to a soul today—someone who needs You as much as I needed You before I came to know You."

If you begin the day with this heart attitude, you will be prepared for whatever God brings across your path. Though you may not directly speak to someone today, you will still share Christ in your actions, because of your open-heart attitude. The key attitude is openness toward God, to whomever He leads you to and for whatever reason. Once you open your heart, keep it open during the day. Paul calls believers to "pray without ceasing." By having this open heart during the day, you will hear God's direction.

Many people are afraid to share their faith—mostly because they're afraid they

won't have the right words to say. Yet God promises in His word that He will sup-
ply all of our needs (Philippians 4:19), and He also promises to give us the words
to say when we need them, if we have an open heart to hear. His words do not come
back empty (Isaiah 55:11).

Read 1 Peter 3:15. With what attitude are we to share with others? How does
your heart attitude compare with this verse?

_____

_____

REVIEW THE DAY

Take a blank piece of paper and write down the story about how you came to
Christ. Then tell that story to a family member or a spouse. Practice it so you are
comfortable with the words; then ask God for opportunities to use the story. When
you present the story, tell it with boldness and confidence in God's leading.

Read 1 Corinthians 7:20–23. How do you feel about the concept of being a
slave to God? Does anything else enslave you? How can you escape that slavery and
become a slave to God? Write down your plans and insight.

_____

_____

Today make a fresh commitment for God to direct your life and use it to tell
others about Jesus. Write a prayer with that commitment below.

_____

_____

What was the most meaningful sentence or Bible verse in this section? Rephrase
that particular sentence or verse as a prayer to God.

_____

_____

_____

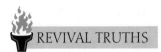

REVIVAL TRUTHS

- Our attitude needs to be open to God's daily will for our lives.
- If we are open to God, He will direct us to those with whom we can share.
- Openness to God begins at the first part of the day.

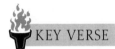

KEY VERSE

But sanctify the Lord God in your hearts: and be ready always to give an answer to every man that asketh you a reason of the hope that is in you with meekness and fear. (1 Peter 3:15)

DAY FOUR

AN AVAILABLE DAY

David McKenna, former president of Asbury Theological Seminary, wrote, "We are a generation of spiritual doers who do not have the time or patience to exercise the spiritual disciplines of "being." As an evangelical activist myself, I realize . . . [that we] minimize prayer and maximize planning." Later, he added, "Jesus' example of working with His disciples and Paul's emphasis on the Body of Christ refute this notion. Our 'being' and 'doing' require mutual accountability in the Christian community as well as personal accountability to God."[5]

How do you plan your time? Do you plan your own time or do the events and urgency of the day plan it for you? Or do you just let it happen—in response to God? It is possible for our days to become so tightly packed with activities that there is no time available to allow a move of God.

How do you plan your schedule? How flexible are you to the moving of God?

_____

_____

Consider how you make decisions about whether to commit to something for yourself or your family. When an opportunity arises, do you stop and ask God's opinion, or do you just say yes because it might sound like a good idea? I'm not talking about hours on our knees, but even just a quick prayer, "God, is this OK with you?" Doing so will give a check in your spirit about His plan.

I've heard this saying: "If the devil can't make you bad, he'll make you busy." We have bought into productivity hook, line, and sinker. Not that being productive is bad. And not that doing good things is wrong. What causes problems is that we're so tied up doing things we thought were a good idea, but were outside the will of

God, that we have no time to respond when God calls us to a specific task. We don't like to wait on God. In our waiting, we often feel "lazy." So we fill our time. But at what expense?

> ### *Revival is . . .*
> *nothing more than a new beginning*
> *of obedience to the Word of God.*
>
> Charles Finney

How do you make decisions about spending your time? Do you think that process honors God?

_____

_____

The Lord told Ezekiel, "And I sought for a man among them, that should make up the hedge, and stand in the gap before me for the land, that I should not destroy it: but I found none" (Ezekiel 22:30). God needs you to stand in the gap for your family, your friends, your neighborhood, your city, your country, and your world. The question is, are you available?

You can pray, "Today, Lord, I want to stand before you. I want to be intimate with you. I want to stand in the gap today. Order my steps so that I am always doing exactly what you want me to be doing."

Do you think Jesus was lazy? Probably not. And yet, He often appeared to take His time in situations we would see as requiring immediate action. Read the story of Lazarus in John 11. One interesting point in this story is that while Lazarus was on his deathbed, Jesus remained away two more days. The events of those two days are so insignificant that John didn't even record them. We know now how the story ends, but at the time it actually happened, no one knew, except Jesus Himself. Jesus was available to be where the Father directed, regardless of the circumstances around Him and what *appeared* to be right. How available are you?

REVIEW THE DAY

God is looking for men and women to stand in the gap for their neighbors and loved ones. How are you standing in the gap? Or how could you be standing in the gap? Write down some ideas in the space below.

_____

_____

As you go through each day, how do you make yourself available for God's use? How are you available to share Him with others?

_____

_____

What's your attitude? How can you be sensitive to others, or busy with your own tasks? What should you look for to know when a person is ready to talk about God? Write about your attitude and level of sensitivity in the space below. How can you grow in this area?

_____

_____

Today make a fresh commitment to analyze your day and have God direct your steps. Write a prayer with that commitment below.

_____

_____

What was the most meaningful sentence or Bible verse in this section? Rephrase that particular sentence or verse as a prayer to God.

_____

_____

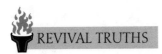

REVIVAL TRUTHS

- Our day can be random or planned.
- It is our responsibility to be available for God's use, regardless of our own plans.
- Our availability often depends on how we consult God before we make a commitment of our time.

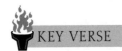

KEY VERSE

And I sought for a man among them, that should make up the hedge, and stand in the gap before me for the land, that I should not destroy it: but I found none. (Ezekiel 22:30)

DAY FIVE

FULL-CYCLE EVANGELISM

Have you ever noticed the motley crew Jesus had as followers? Most of them were poor peasants—generally farmers and fishermen. He had Judas, a money-grabbing traitor; Peter, a swaggering, egotistical braggart, always getting his foot in his mouth when he should have been silent; James and John, ambitious boys who eventually would try hard for the top seats in the kingdom. He also had Matthew, a despised Roman tax collector. He even had at least one prostitute, as well as some other women of questionable reputations. What a hopeless group on which to build a kingdom of purity, modesty, humility, and holy principles! Not a one with any moral sense.

Who would have expected anything but ignominious defeat and disastrous ruin of this group once it lost its charming and powerful leader? But Christ welded this disparate crowd into a Spirit-filled, power-baptized, evangelizing, crusading, martyr-making, world-shaking organization. The group would conquer kingdoms, lifting putrid civilizations out of their despair and ruins onto the high plateaus of nobility and usefulness. Eventually, His followers through the centuries would redeem people by the millions!

God expects no less from us, broken sinners that we are. As Peter and John carried the message of Christ, we too are called to carry the message of Christ. Our purpose to share the good news is for salvation, but there is a second purpose. Read Matthew 28:19. What is the commandment of Christ?

_____

_____

Jesus spent years with these men and women during His time of ministry. The

197

heart of the purpose of Jesus' relationship with the disciples can be found in John 15:15–16. Read those verses and summarize them here.

_____

_____

Based on those verses, what is our purpose in discipling others?

_____

_____

> *Revival and evangelism, although closely linked, are not be to confused. Revival is an experience in the Church; evangelism is an expression of the Church.*
>
> —<>—
>
> Paul S. Rees

Often the word *disciple* can be even more intimidating than the word *evangelism.* Part of the reason is discipleship takes a bigger commitment, something we are often reluctant to do. The word *disciple* means "learner." It's impossible to learn from someone without an investment on the part of both the pupil and the teacher. Jesus' example was one of total devotion to those who would believe and follow. Does God ask any less of us?

What is your commitment to disciple others who have come to Christ?

_____

_____

Full-cycle evangelism is helping those who accept Christ to grow in maturity so they can share their faith with others. We are saved not just for our benefit, but to share with others. Read Romans 10:13–15. How does this relate to our responsibility to discipleship?

_____

_____

As people make commitments to Christ, we must love them enough to say, "Could we meet once a month (or once a week) to simply go through a basic Bible study together?" Some great Bible studies are available to use in follow-up. (See the Resource page for several published by International Students.) Someone who is brand new in the faith can use these studies to help someone else grow in their relationship with Christ.

You need to be willing to sacrifice. Remember the sixth point from Charles Finney —to sacrifice whatever God requires (see day two). That sacrifice most often is in the form of time and love.

REVIEW THE DAY

What barriers do you have to break down related to discipleship?

_____

_____

Today make a new commitment for God to use you in discipleship. Write a prayer with that commitment below.

_____

_____

What was the most meaningful sentence or Bible verse in this section? Rephrase that particular sentence or verse as a prayer to God.

_____

_____

_____

What action does God want you to take as a result of today's study? Meditate, think deeply, and listen to your heart; then write about the action you will take.

_____

_____

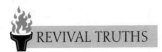
REVIVAL TRUTHS

- God uses unlikely characters to spread His Gospel.
- We are called not just to evangelism, but discipleship.
- Discipleship requires sacrifice and commitment.

KEY VERSE

For whosoever shall call upon the name of the Lord shall be saved. How then shall they call on him in whom they have not believed? and how shall they believe in him of whom they have not heard? and how shall they hear without a preacher? And how shall they preach, except they be sent? as it is written, How beautiful are the feet of them that preach the gospel of peace, and bring glad tidings of good things! (Romans 10:13–15)

LOOKING AHEAD

As we see the results of revival—evangelism—we see a little more of our part in God's plan. In chapter 9, we'll discover how God uses the past, the present, and even the future to work together for His unfolding plan.

9 A KEY TIME IN SPIRITUAL HISTORY

At the end of the twentieth century, Campus Crusade President Bill Bright pointed to four elements coming together for a worldwide movement of God's Spirit and worldwide evangelistic outreach. Those four have never existed in prior Christian church endeavors, according to Bright. They are: strategy, resources, technology, and people.[1]

1. Strategy. We have a plan for worldwide evangelism that has come from prayer and evangelistic movements, including AD 2000 and Beyond, and Mission America.
2. Resources. We've got more money in Christian hands than ever before. In the United States alone, for funding Christian ventures, $13 trillion will change hands in the next decade from one generation to the next, Bright reported. Also, in the midst of this potential funding, the resourcing agencies and individuals are gathering together to more effectively distribute their funding. These groups meet regularly, meet the mission and ministry agencies, allow them to share what they are doing, and then proceed to invest. Never before has this occurred in the history of the Christian church.
3. Technology. We've never had the opportunity to communicate around the world so inexpensively and so quickly. The claims of Christ can be spread quickly through television, radio, and the Internet.

4. People. Many Christians are coming together in vocational service to God. For example, since 1998, men and women have attended the Finishers Conferences, designed for workers who want to move from success to significance with their lives. Those attending have arrived at midlife of their career and are considering a move to using their skills with Christian agencies. A good tool for you to learn more about how to make this movement in your own life is *Halftime,* by Bob Buford (Zondervan). Similarly, for years Intercristo has helped Christians at any point in their careers find opportunities to work full time with Christian ministries.

Bill Bright has described several key elements that are converging in the church today. These converging elements may bring about the greatest spiritual awakening the world has ever expereinced, for these converging revival streams are more powerful that any seen previously. God is preparing us for a great awakening.

DAY ONE

LESSONS
FROM THE PAST

In 1858 the United States was in turmoil. The economy was weak. One of the major political parties was dissolving over the slavery issue. Civil War was imminent. Detractors believed, with good cause, that America would not survive.

During this time, one of the old churches in New York City, the old North Dutch Church, was also in a desperate condition. The church had lost its constituency. People had moved away. The leadership of the church could not even find an ordained clergy to pastor the fleeing congregation.

A New York businessman named Jeremiah Lanphier was invited to lead the church. Not knowing what to do, he developed handbills and distributed them throughout the area to businesspeople, inviting them for prayer on Thursdays. The initial meeting began at twelve o'clock and no one arrived until 12:30. By 1 o'clock six people had become a part of this meeting. The next week twenty gathered, the following week, forty. Within six months thousands of people were gathering at lunch to pray for the nation. The newspapers covered the meetings. The press accounts flowed, and the stories were inspiring. Here are two, as recounted in *America's Great Revivals*.

One time a man wandered into the Fulton Street meeting who intended to murder a woman and then commit suicide. He listened as someone was delivering a fervent exhortation and urging the duty of repentance. Suddenly the would-be murderer startled everyone by crying out, "Oh! What shall I do to be saved!" Just then another man arose and with tears streaming down his cheeks asked the meeting to sing the hymn, "Rock of Ages, Cleft for Me." At the conclusion of the service both men were converted.

Another time an aged pastor got up to pray for the son of another clergyman. Unknown to him, his own son was sitting some distance behind him. The young man, knowing himself to be a sinner, was so impressed hearing his father pray for another man's son that he made himself known to the meeting and said he wanted to submit to God.[2]

Within two years, one million people had made commitments to Christ through this lay-led prayer movement that spread from New York into other cities in the nation, often filling every public building at lunch day after day, Monday through Friday. Professional ministers were on the sidelines. People were reaching the heart of God.[3]

> *In revival the things of heaven become all important,*
> *the things of earth of much less importance.*
>
> Anonymous

Yet, surprisingly little has been written about Jeremiah C. Lanphier. At a time of national turmoil and uncertainty, God chose a most unlikely prospect and a most unlikely church to lead one of the greatest works in the history of this nation.
Read Isaiah 55:8–9. How do God's ways compare with our ways?

_____

_____

What lessons in your own life show God's ways as higher than your own?

_____

_____

God uses "the foolish things of the world to confound the wise," the apostle Paul wrote (1 Corinthians 1:27). Although you may feel foolish or unworthy to be used of God, history is clear that God will use unlikely people to bring about great change. Do not underestimate the power of God to work His will in His own way.
The Prayer Revival of 1858 was a climax of great political, social, economic, and spiritual desperation. The concerted prayer touched God's heart. God brought those two circumstances—a time of desperate need and of concerted prayer—together for revival among the people, and used an ordinary man in the process.

REVIEW THE DAY

Are you an unlikely vessel for God? Why or why not?

_____

_____

Read 1 Corinthians 1:25–31. Summarize an application of those verses to your life.

_____

_____

Are you willing to trust God to use you in any way He desires? What prevents that trust? Write a prayer offering yourself to God's plan—no matter what it is.

_____

_____

Today make a fresh commitment to see God work in your life day in and day out. Write a prayer with that commitment below.

_____

_____

What was the most meaningful sentence or Bible verse in this section? Rephrase that particular sentence or verse as a prayer to God.

_____

_____

_____

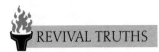

REVIVAL TRUTHS

- God's ways are different from our ways.
- God chooses unlikely people to carry out His plan.
- We choose to submit to God's desire to use us.

KEY VERSE

But God hath chosen the foolish things of the world to confound the wise; and God hath chosen the weak things of the world to confound the things which are mighty. (1 Corinthians 1:27)

DAY TWO

THE CURRENT CLIMAX

When we talk about the move of the Holy Spirit today, consider the following recent headlines and reports:[4]

- "Sikhs come to Faith in Vancouver"
- "Billy Graham Preaches on Revival in Tampa Bay." At the conclusion of a special concert, Graham told the mostly teenage crowd: "I hope that all of you will be in the spirit of prayer, that we will see a mighty outpouring of the Spirit of God. If it happens, the news of it will reach all over the country. God is speaking to us and saying we need revival—from the President on down."
- "Youth Crying Out to God in Tulsa, Oklahoma"
- "Unexpected Baptisms in the Sudan"
- "Evangelism Strategies Going into Place in Central Africa"
- "Massive Rates of Christian Conversion in Korea, China, Taiwan, and Indonesia." The article estimated 25 percent of the Korean population is now Christian, and 40 million people in China are Christian, up from one million in 1980.[5]
- One-third of teens, 35 percent, said that religious faith was the "most important" influence in their lives in a The Religious Research Center survey.[6]
- More than 90 percent of the people in Almolonga, Guatemala, are now evangelical Christians.[7]

We didn't hear of such powerful news events happening fifteen years ago.

Of course, opposition to the Spirit of God still thrives. It's happening all over the world, from arrests of house church leaders in Shenghou, China, where nine leaders were interrogated—some were tortured; others were sentenced to labor camps—to even here in the United States. Consider just this headline: "Coach Fired for Praying for the Team." The accompanying story explained that a Little League coach in Hollywood, Florida, was fired for praying with his team. League board member Ted Dudash told a wire service reporter that he warned the coach that prayer would not be tolerated. Coach Mike Lindell later said, "These kids want to pray, and I am not going to tell them they can't. It's a basic right. People have to start realizing that prayer does not hurt them, it helps. It's not a bad thing."[8]

Consider your world today. Is there an open door for the move of God's Spirit, or is opposition seemingly keeping the door closed?

_____

_____

Is your heart open to the move of God's Spirit, or do you have roadblocks? If so, describe them here. Pray that God would show you how to release them.

_____

_____

There are five obvious areas in which America is ready for spiritual revival:

1. The Holy Spirit is being poured out in obvious ways.
2. Prayer is increasing in significant numbers and frequency.
3. Unity is sweeping biblical Christianity.
4. Brokenness is spreading among believers.
5. Among the church population, more people are becoming warriors for God.

> ### Revival is . . .
> *nothing more than a*
> *return to Apostolic Christianity.*
>
> —⊷◈⊶—
>
> John Morgan

The twentieth century will be known as "The Martyrs' Century," as several mission agencies have reported that more people have lost their lives for their Christian faith during the century just concluded than in the previous nineteen centuries combined. Most of those martyrs were not Americans. And yet, we in the United States often see ourselves as "superior, more spiritual" Christians because of our culture and lifestyle. If we are children of God, following God's Word with the Holy Spirit as our Guide, then we have to die to our own traditions that lift up our egos and self above others.

During a major prayer conference involving more than one hundred organizational leaders in November 1998, Bob Reccord, president of the mission board of the Southern Baptist Convention, stood up and said, "I pray as we come in these doors today, we have left our logos and our egos at the door because we come here as servant leaders of this nation to bow before God almighty and ask Him to move through us in unity to reach a lost and dying world."

Never before have all of these points converged into a single stream of activity —resources, people, strategy, or technology. God has promised a "new thing" and He is pouring out His Spirit now. Get under the downpour.

REVIEW THE DAY

Read Esther 4. The circumstances of Esther's day were grave for the Jewish people. Please summarize the situation. (You may need to read more of Esther.)

_____

_____

What was Esther's role?

_____

_____

How does her role compare with your role for today?

_____

_____

A KEY TIME IN SPIRITUAL HISTORY

This reading—and the chapter—discuss how God is bringing together the events of human history. Why is it important to see this pattern in God's work?

_____

_____

Study Isaiah 30:15–26. What aspects of the moving of God's Spirit today do you see in this passage?

_____

_____

How do you experience the work of the Holy Spirit in your life?

_____

_____

Today make a fresh commitment to increase your awareness of how world events are coming together in a unique fashion. Ask God to reveal this awareness to you. Write a prayer with that commitment below.

_____

_____

What was the most meaningful sentence or Bible verse in this section? Rephrase that particular sentence or verse as a prayer to God.

_____

_____

_____

What action does God want you to take as a result of today's study? Meditate, think deeply, and listen to your heart; then write about the action you will take.

_____

_____

REVIVAL TRUTHS

- God is working in a fresh way to bring together the course of human events for His Kingdom.
- There is both openness and opposition to the move of God's Spirit.

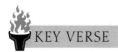

KEY VERSE

Therefore the Lord will wait, that He may be gracious to you; and therefore He will be exalted, that He may have mercy on you. For the Lord is a God of justice; blessed are all those who wait for Him. (Isaiah 30:18 NKJV)

DAY THREE

HOPE FOR
THE FUTURE

Interestingly, headlines in various newspapers and magazines recently have been most encouraging as we begin to see a shift in our nation. Perhaps, as George Gallup told a gathering of Christian leaders in Colorado Springs in the fall of 1998, "The pendulum in America has already begun to swing, from materialism to spirituality, but it's a free-floating spirituality looking for a place to light."[9]

Hope for the future lies in the relationship that today's young people are developing with Jesus Christ. We see youth today standing up for God, even to the point of death. The Columbine High School shootings remain a vivid example. On April 20, 1999, two high school students killed twelve students, one teacher, and themselves. How could God work in this situation? Through this tragedy that rocked the nation, Christian students like Cassie Bernall and John Tomblin Jr. stood firm in their faith in Christ. Gunmen who professed to follow Satan had targeted Christians and others.

"Do you believe in God?" one of the shooters asked Cassie Bernall.

"Yes, I believe in Jesus Christ," she replied.

"Why?" he asked. Cassie was murdered before she could reply.

But physical death did not shut the voice of this young martyr. Weeks and months later, students wore T-shirts with Cassie Bernall's picture, inscribed, "Yes, I believe." These students said, "We'll take our high school back for God." They're answering the question which the misled young executioner asked, a question parents and adult society has not adequately responded to: "Why?"

There is hope that though Cassie and her classmates may be the first of many martyrs to come in the United States, the message of Jesus is being gripped by a new generation in a way the current generation never imagined.

> *Send Your fire,*
> *Send Your rain,*
> *Holy oil in Jesus' name.*
> *Loose the wind*
> *That brings Heaven's change:*
> *Send the fire,*
> *Send the oil,*
> *The wind and rain.*
>
> —◆—
>
> "SEND YOUR FIRE"/Kent Henry

Age is not a factor when it comes to living a godly life. Timothy was a fellow traveler and official representative for the apostle Paul, even though he was much younger than Paul. Paul exhorted Timothy to continue with the ministry, to be bold, even though he was young (read 1 Timothy 4:11–16). Timothy was faithful and obedient even though he was shy and reserved. The question for adults today is: Can we willingly pass the torch to this new generation? Are we willing to humbly step aside and allow God's future to come to pass?

Why is entrusting a new generation with God's mission difficult for some leaders? Is that a godly attitude?

_____

_____

On any Sunday at New Life Church, the largest church in Colorado Springs (average attendance of about 6,000), hundreds of youth stand at the altar during the praise-and-worship part of the service. These youth not only praise God openly, they live each day in the same manner. These are not timid children who sing "Jesus Loves Me" once a week during a youth meeting. These are bold teens leading Bible studies in their schools, studying Christian apologetics, and sacrificing for the cause of Christ. Some have made trips to closed countries in order to drop Gospel tracts; others have fed the hungry, helped the disabled, and reached out to the lost youth in their city.

It's true, the youth of today don't look like the youth of my day. Their hair is sometimes purple and they have earrings in places I couldn't imagine. Does it mean they love Jesus less? I don't think so. Does it mean they are less called into His service? No. No more than it meant John Wesley had lost his faith by rewriting "bar" tunes of the day with Christian lyrics. God moves in each generation. Perhaps we would better serve today's youth to come alongside them to support their ministry. While they can learn from us, we can also learn from them.

The next generation is taking up the cross of Jesus with an intensity and purpose unmatched. We can have hope in our future.

REVIEW THE DAY

Do you see the future as hopeful? Why or why not?

_____

_____

Do you have difficulty accepting the faith of young people who don't always look the Christian part? Pray now and ask God to help you see them through His eyes. Write your response.

_____

_____

How do you see God's purposes being fulfilled in your children, or the children of those around you?

_____

_____

Pick a young person who inspires you. Describe what is inspirational about that teenager. Pray for that person.

_____

_____

What was the most meaningful sentence or Bible verse in this section? Rephrase that particular sentence or verse as a prayer to God.

_____

_____

_____

What action does God want you to take as a result of today's study? Meditate, think deeply, and listen to your heart; then write about the action you will take.

_____

_____

REVIVAL TRUTHS

- God will continue to work in the future as He has worked in the past and present.
- Today's youth are committed to Christ.
- Adults can walk alongside the youth to support them in their ministry.
- We have hope for the future because of the youth of today.

KEY VERSE

And it shall come to pass afterward, that I will pour out my spirit upon all flesh; and your sons and your daughters shall prophesy, your old men shall dream dreams, your young men shall see visions. (Joel 2:28)

DAY FOUR

WHAT DOES GOD PROMISE?

During a recent International Student youth retreat in Austin, Texas, I chatted with a twenty-seven year old with a Ph.D. in computer science. He had returned from China, where he had been making $100,000 a year with a Chinese company—an extraordinary amount in that country. Five weeks before the retreat, Mr. Zhao accepted Christ, quit his job, and came back to the U.S. to study the Bible with the goal of taking the Gospel to China. Talk about choice. I sat with this young Christian, mesmerized at his faith in the promises of God.

Zhao told me, "I can see only about a year into my future, but I know my God can see the rest of my life." He had been sleeping on a couch in an apartment with two other believers in Austin, wanting to get into a Bible college or seminary and learn about God. This man had come from nothing, achieved worldly wealth and success, and then made a choice to give it up to serve the Lord.

What does God promise Zhao? What does He promise us? Consider just a few of the promises of God.

- *He is worthy of our trust.* "Commit thy way unto the Lord; trust also in him; and he shall bring it to pass" (Psalm 37:5).
- *He gives mercy.* "Not by works of righteousness which we have done, but according to his mercy he saved us, by the washing of regeneration, and renewing of the Holy Ghost" (Titus 3:5).
- *He offers forgiveness.* "Forbearing one another, and forgiving one another, if any man have a quarrel against any: even as Christ forgave you, so also do ye" (Colossians 3:13).
- *He has great love.* "We love him, because he first loved us" (1 John 4:19).

216

- *He gives strength.* "I can do all things through Christ which strengtheneth me" (Philippians 4:13).
- *He protects us from fear.* "What time I am afraid, I will trust in thee" (Psalm 56:3).
- *He gives guidance.* "Thy word is a lamp unto my feet, and a light unto my path" (Psalm 119:105).
- *He will never forsake us.* "For he hath said, I will never leave thee, nor forsake thee" (Hebrews 13:5).
- *He gives peace.* "And the peace of God, which passeth all understanding, shall keep your hearts and minds through Christ Jesus" (Philippians 4:7).

Mr. Zhao was willing to step out in faith, to test God, to see if God was true. His reward of knowing the faithfulness of God will be great. If we are not willing to step out in faith, to go wherever God leads, we may never know the depth of His promises for us.

Read 2 Corinthians 1:20. What has God promised you and me?

_____

_____

Have you allowed God to put you in a position where you must depend on His promises? Explain.

_____

_____

Search the Scriptures for three more promises of God. List those here.

_____

_____

_____

God promises that all will have the opportunity to know Him. In the Muslim world, dreams are greatly respected. One woman had a dream that troubled her. When this woman was a teenager, her father had been a Christian but in the subsequent years had left his faith. Several years later, this woman had a dream and a being appeared who called himself Issa (the Arabic word for Jesus) saying, "Follow me."

The next day, the woman went to her father and asked, "Who is Issa?"

He said, "Well . . . that's God."

"And this Issa told me to follow him. What does that mean?"

"Well, that's God speaking to you."

Not satisfied with his answers, the woman persisted in seeking God for years. Finally she went to a Christian man whom she knew and asked about her dream. He explained the story of young Samuel who served in the temple. When the Lord called to Samuel, he called out and said, "Lord, what do you want to say to me?" (See 1 Samuel 3:8–10.) This Christian advised the woman to follow a similar course of action.

The dream never occurred again, but in the following months, this woman came to believe in Jesus Christ because she knew about Issa. God keeps His promises.

Revival is . . .

above everything else, a glorification of the Lord Jesus Christ, the Son of God. It is the restoration of him to the centre of the life of the Church.

—◆—

D.M. Lloyd-Jones

 REVIEW THE DAY

God's promises are precious to us. Return to several of the promises in the section above. Plan to memorize these verses and keep these words from God in your heart. Which verse will you memorize first? Plan it below and be specific.

_____

_____

Is there an area of your life that God is calling you to step out in faith, to trust that His promises are true? If so, list it below. How can you step out in faith?

_____

_____

What was the most meaningful sentence or Bible verse in this section? Rephrase that particular sentence or verse as a prayer to God.

_____

_____

_____

What action does God want you to take as a result of today's study? Meditate, think deeply, and listen to your heart; then write about the action you will take.

_____

_____

_____

REVIVAL TRUTHS

- God's promises are precious and true.
- We must step out in faith to see the deep faithfulness of God.

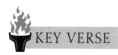

KEY VERSE

For all the promises of God in Him are Yes, and in Him Amen, to the glory of God through us. (2 Corinthians 1:20 NKJV)

DAY FIVE

FACADES

Have you ever visited a movie set or seen the backside of a stage set? What looks like an actual building from the front is proven to be nothing more than a facade. There is no real house or western street. There is no security or shelter in a facade. Just a painted front held by a few two-by-fours for the duration of the play or movie. It doesn't take much to knock it over once the production is complete. It wasn't real to begin with.

Many believers today hold onto facades in their lives. Even though they have seen God at work in the past, and see Him at work today, they are not able to hold onto His promises for a new generation and the future. Consider some facades you might cling to: control, self-preservation, an "I can do it myself, thank you" attitude, self-competence, an unhealthy dependence on a relationship, your income level, the neighborhood in which you live, your kid's school, the kind of car you drive, the church you attend . . . . The list goes on.

Perhaps there are facades in your life. Think about it for a moment: What do you cling to in place of God?

_____

_____

Why are these facades?

_____

_____

> *I have learned to know beyond the shadow of doubt,*
> *that the will of God is the most delicious and*
> *delightful thing in the universe.*
>
> —————
>
> Hannah Whitall Smith

Read Matthew 7:21–27. Notice the verses that immediately precede this familiar story. Jesus had been warning His listeners to watch out for false prophets who appear to be sheep, but are actually wolves (see especially verse 15). They are like buildings with facades. Jesus explained that not everyone who appears to know God actually does. True followers of Christ are known by their fruit.

What kind of fruit does your life bear? Are you satisfied with it? Do you think God is?

_____

_____

"Sue" came to work for International Students, Inc. after a successful job where she supervised more than one hundred people and earned a substantial salary. She left a ten-year career and financial success because she felt a call to full-time ministry and wanted to obey. In the process, she saw her income take a nosedive, and her position of responsibility was diminished. Though she felt at peace, there was a raw ache within her.

Eventually, Sue realized that she had derived all of her worth as a person from her job, her income, her position of control. She depended on a facade of stability when she needed to depend on God. Through prayer and honesty with God, He showed her a better way. He reminded her of Ephesians 1:3–6, which declared that God loved her and chose her before He laid the foundation of the world. It didn't matter whether she was a top executive or a janitor, what mattered was God's love for her, and her obedience to His call. The facades had been broken down. God could build a real structure now.

REVIEW THE DAY

Revival is possible only when we are focused and devoted to God. Any facade we hold creates a form of idol worship, and revival cannot come without our hearts worshipping God alone.

Read Matthew 7:23–27 again. What kind of ground is your life built upon—sand or rock?

_____

_____

Read Ephesians 1. What is our inheritance? Why is that better than the facades we cling to?

_____

_____

Pray now and ask God to convict you of anything you hold onto beside Him. What is His response?

_____

_____

Make a commitment to seek God for your needs, not the facades in your life. Write that prayer of commitment.

_____

_____

What was the most meaningful sentence or Bible verse in this section? Rephrase that particular sentence or verse as a prayer to God.

_____

_____

_____

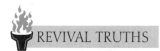

REVIVAL TRUTHS

- We often depend on facades rather than the power of God.
- God cannot work through us when we cling to facades.
- God is willing to help us expose and remove those facades.

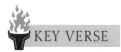

KEY VERSE

Therefore whosoever heareth these sayings of mine, and doeth them, I will liken him unto a wise man, which built his house upon a rock. (Matthew 7:24)

LOOKING AHEAD

God is always at work. He never sleeps. He has worked in the past, is working in the present, and will continue to work in the future. Ours is to embrace His will and work. Let's look ahead to God's specific work in our nation.

10 GOD'S WORK IN OUR NATION

Our nation has few spiritual moorings left. In a 1962 U.S. Supreme Court decision, prayer was removed from the public schools. Today "Merry Christmas" has become "happy holidays." "Jesus Christ" is rarely heard other than as a curse. Even A.D., which stands for *anno Domini*, "in the year of the Lord," is being replaced by C.E., or "of the common era," to show the current year. Yes, we are a country with minimal spiritual anchors. Charlie Jarvis, an attorney and the previous executive vice president of Focus on the Family, said, "If God is gone, all things are permissible."

The Bible says, "Righteousness exalteth a nation: but sin is a reproach to any people" (Proverbs 14:34). It's not that "being good" exalts a nation per se, but rather that principles of righteous behavior lead to national success. God put these in place at the foundation of the world, knowing that loving, biblical principles would be the best help to people in their relationships with each other and with God.

In 1998, researcher and trend forecaster George Barna spoke to nearly two hundred pastors in Colorado Springs. One of the pastors asked George what he thought was going to happen in our nation. The noted commentator and author thought solemnly for a moment, and then responded, "We are either going to have revival within the next ten years, or we are going to have anarchy."

After a moment of thoughtful silence, the pastor asked, "George, which do you think it will be?"

"I believe it will be anarchy," Barna replied.[1] There was complete silence throughout the room as the pastors wondered at his response. Barna believes in God and in revival. He even wrote the preface for my previous book, *Revival Signs.* Why would he choose anarchy?

The pastor pressed George for a reason.

"I'm not God," the pollster responded. "Revival is in the hands of God, and only He can see what He is going to do, but, if He doesn't intervene in the affairs of this nation, we shall have anarchy."

Revival happens one person at a time. Because of that, the fate of the nation may literally hinge on how Christians maintain their walk with Christ. God can flow to the lost through His church. As others come to Christ and begin to grow through consistent time in God's Word, His truth will speak to the renewed heart and increase a burden for social justice.

Remember, society is changed from the inside out to conform to God's Word. Revival is the precursor to explosive salvation of the lost, and that is the precursor to social justice.

DAY ONE

WHO IS IN CHARGE
OF THE NATION?

William Penn once talked about the fact that if you won't have God, you will have tyrants. In the midst of the darkness of our nation, we wonder if it is spinning out of control. What do we believe? Is God in charge? Consider just a few of the ills our country faces:

- We see a general disrespect for life through abortion, child abuse, and euthanasia.
- AIDS is an epidemic.
- Crime remains a serious problem.
- Divorce remains rampant.
- Inner cities are in chaos and decline.
- Workplace ethics are questionable at best.
- Truth is relative.
- Moral foundations, once embraced, now are crumbling.

The pessimist would look at our nation and say we don't have a prayer. The truth is that prayer is all we do have. It's our hope.

> *Study the history of revival.*
> *God has always sent revival in the darkest days.*
> *Oh for a mighty sweeping revival today.*
>
> ———
>
> Adrian Rogers

And yet, as we enter the twenty-first century, people in the United States have a growing and intense interest in spiritual matters and biblical prophecy. Tim La-Haye and Jerry B. Jenkins have written a series of novels about the end times before Christ's final return called the Left Behind series. This wildly popular series has sold a combined total of more than 11 million copies, crossing into the secular markets and showing people's desire to know about their spiritual future. It's not just end-of-the-world information people seek, but truth. Consider these article titles, from the pages of America's leading news magazines:

- "Finding God"; *Newsweek* magazine
- "Jesus of Nazareth"; *Time*
- "Dark Prophecies"; *U. S. News & World Report*[2]

When considering the dawn of a new millennium, Bill Bright, president of Campus Crusade, wrote, "I'm standing on tip-toe with anticipation to see a great spiritual tidal wave sweep our land and envelope our whole globe. Our Lord came to seek and save the lost."[3]

Yes, God is in charge, just as He always has been. Consider the ministry of Habakkuk. For decades, this Old Testament prophet prayed for his nation only to see it slip further into a moral abyss, spiritual lethargy. But God reminded Habakkuk of His involvement and promised His ways would continue: "For the earth shall be filled with the knowledge of the glory of the Lord, as the waters cover the sea. He stood, and measured the earth: he beheld, and drove asunder the nations; and the everlasting mountains were scattered, the perpetual hills did bow: his ways are everlasting" (Habakkuk 2:14, 3:6). God was—and is—in charge. In the midst of corruption, God was still in command.

In contrast, Isaiah did not doubt the mighty hand of God: "Oh that thou wouldest rend the heavens, that thou wouldest come down, that the mountains might flow down at thy presence, . . . to make thy name known to thine adversaries, that the nations may tremble at thy presence!" (Isaiah 64:1–2). Any question about the omnipotence of God?

Are you convinced in your heart that God is in charge of all situations? If so, does your prayer life reflect this conviction? If not, explain why you doubt.

Why is it difficult to trust God's control when circumstances look grim?

_____

_____

Search for five other Scriptures that demonstrate God's power and control in all circumstances. Write their references below.

_____

_____

As a nation, Americans have not turned their hearts toward God; because of that, we suffer consequences. God's power to redeem, however, is never diminished. In the midst of our chaos is His peace and hope. In 1994, two Christian leaders were part of a private briefing with the President. Walking across the White House lawn after the meeting, one said to the other, "If God doesn't send revival, nothing else really matters." He meant that spiritual renewal for the country is necessary. Otherwise, we're hopelessly lost.

The other leader responded, "And, if God does send revival, nothing else really matters."[4] A spiritual awakening of America can and will turn this nation upside down.

REVIEW THE DAY

Read Psalm 74:12. What hope do you find in this verse?

_____

_____

What in current events do you see as a sign of God's movement in our nation? Write down at least one example.

_____

_____

How do these current events increase your hope, faith and prayers? Write a prayer with that commitment below.

_____

_____

What was the most meaningful sentence or Bible verse in this section? Rephrase that particular sentence or verse as a prayer to God.

_____

_____

What action does God want you to take as a result of today's study? Meditate, think deeply, and listen to your heart; then write about the action you will take.

_____

_____

 REVIVAL TRUTHS

- God is moving in a fresh way in our country.
- God is in charge, despite negative circumstances.

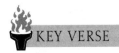 KEY VERSE

For God is my King of old, working salvation in the midst of the earth. (Psalm 74:12)

DAY TWO

LIVING LIKE
GOD IS IN CHARGE

Our country has reached a critical juncture, and it's time for courage, boldness, and speaking the truth. You may feel insignificant, but you'll never know how God will use you until you obey the burden He places on your heart. If we believe God is in charge, then we respond to His call, knowing it is for His purpose to be accomplished.

Each of us can and should respond. For Carolyn McKenzie and Marnie Ferree, the responses came to the ongoing threat our country faces from pornography and sexual addiction. These women didn't lead any organization or rise from a position of national power. They simply responded to a concern through the power of God. They are living like God is in charge.

A public health nurse, Carolyn organized protests and filed complaints with the district attorney about the porn shops and strip clubs in suburban Memphis. Some people called McKenzie a hypocrite because she was fighting to close places she had never been inside. To handle this objection, McKenzie asked a vice cop for a tour of the seamier side of Memphis. This policeman took her to "modeling agencies" and topless clubs. "I felt so discouraged," Carolyn recalled, "like there was no way I could ever begin to affect this industry." It was then she noticed the dancers. "I was actually surprised to find out there are actually clean-cut college or career girls. A lot of them are doing it simply because they need the money."[5] So she started leading these young ladies to Christ and helping them find other options to escape the sex industry.

"I look at these girls as the daughter I never had," she said. She organized a group called the Memphis Citizens for Community Values, which uses mentors from local churches to help dancers leave the industry—that means providing the assistance they need to make a break—including paying their bills, helping them find jobs, and arranging free counseling and medical care.

Meanwhile, Marnie Ferree of Nashville works with sexually addicted women. Once caught in the web herself, Marnie has created a twelve-step support group to help heal the addiction. "There really is such a thing as sexual addiction. It's not just a male disease." Her addiction cost her her marriage. "I kept doing what I didn't want to do," she explained. That's the classic definition of addiction, and she traces the root of her sexual addiction to early childhood, when a twenty-year-old family friend molested her (Marnie was only five at the time), and the abuse continued for years. As a teen, she became promiscuous and later married. Through the help of a Christian therapist and a twelve-step support group, she returned to God.

"I came to know and serve the God who has changed my life. It's only through dependence on God that I'm able to assist these women." Today Ferree has a master's degree in counseling and works professionally with women through Woodmont Hills Counseling Ministry in Nashville. "For me, it's a visible sign of God's grace: He's taken my pain and sin, and He's using me to help others."[6]

Another woman making a difference in her world is Beth Kraiss. Beth works through her local church to reach out to the severely disabled and indigent. Each Sunday morning, hundreds of severely disabled people are picked up from nursing homes and other places in Colorado Springs and driven to New Life Church, where they participate in the praise and worship part of the service. Then they attend classes where they receive a meal, teaching about Jesus, and love. Married for more than thirty years and the mother of two grown daughters, she does the ministry believing everyone has a right to know Jesus. As director of the program, Beth works hard to make sure this group of "unlovables" is loved and cared for.[7]

Like these women, we can participate in God's plan. When we do, we too will see the Spirit of God actively at work, and we will know He is more powerful than the evil we fight in the world.

> *I am only one; but still I am one.*
> *I cannot do everything, but still I can do something.*
> *I will not refuse to do the something I can do.*
>
> Helen Keller

Why is it difficult to stand against evil if you don't believe God is in charge?

Are there situations in which you feel God is calling you to take a stand? List them.

_____

_____

Why is it important to realize God's control in all situations?

_____

_____

REVIEW THE DAY

The Bible is filled with the stories of individuals who made a difference in their communities and world. Take a few minutes and read about one of these heroes: Samson (Judges 13–15), Ruth (Ruth 1–4), or Daniel (Daniel 1–2). These individuals were not perfect, but they still had a positive impact. In the space below write a few words about how they made a difference in their world.

_____

_____

Today ask God to use you in faith to make a difference in your world. Write a prayer with that commitment below.

_____

_____

Read Hebrews 11. Why was faith such a vital characteristic of those mentioned?

_____

_____

What was the most meaningful sentence or Bible verse in this section? Rephrase that particular sentence or verse as a prayer to God.

_____

_____

_____

What action does God want you to take to make a difference as a result of to-day's study? Meditate, think deeply, and listen to your heart; then write about the action you will take.

_____

_____

 REVIVAL TRUTHS

- We are to live our lives knowing God is in charge.
- God uses individuals who walk by faith to make a difference in their world.
- We make a difference by obeying God and reaching one person at a time for Christ.

 KEY VERSE

Through faith we understand that the worlds were framed by the word of God, so that things which are seen were not made of things which do appear. (Hebrews 11:3)

DAY THREE

GOD'S POWER IN OUR NATION

Historically, we have seen God's Spirit in our nation. These outpourings of God's Spirit and power are revealed in a pattern from history and give us reason to anticipate revival. The current events in our nation show the spiritual darkness that cloaks us. In the middle of this darkness, people are looking for light. That light for the soul of a man or woman is found in a relationship with Jesus Christ. Many people are looking for such a relationship because they have had a cracked or broken relationship—out of the brokenness of the world.

The First Great Awakening in the United States prior to the American Revolution (during the early 1730s through 1760s) remains an example of national renewal and revival. Repentance, fasting, and prayer drew the nation to the Lord, releasing mercy, grace, and a withholding of judgment. Later, during the early 1790s, most denominations were shrinking in numbers, and alcoholism was rampant even in children as young as age eleven. This preceded the Second Great Awakening, again triggered by repentance, fasting, and prayer.

As we examine the heritage of our nation, especially the founding fathers, we see that they came to this country for freedom to worship Christ. American President John Adams said, "The general principles in which the fathers achieved independence were . . . the general principles of Christianity. Now I will avow that I then believed and now believe, that those general principles of Christianity are as eternal and immutable as the existence and attributes of God." Benjamin Franklin said, "Whoever shall introduce into public affairs the principles of primitive Christianity will change the face of the world." And the patriot Patrick Henry, best known for declaring, "Give me liberty or give me death," also said, "It cannot be emphasized too strongly or too often that this great nation was founded not by religionists, but by Christians, not on religions, but on the Gospel of Jesus."[8]

255

Clearly, our nation has strayed from this Christian foundation. Its citizens have adopted personal gain as their modern creed. For instance, in a recent article entitled "The Cheating Game," *U. S. News & World Report* writers concluded that when it comes to cheating, "Everyone's doing it."[9]

The family unit is in disarray. In a survey of 1,523 U.S. adults, *CNN/Time* found that 69 percent know a married man who has committed adultery; 60 percent know a married woman who has committed adultery.[10] Spousal abuse, both emotional and physical, is increasingly common, as is child abuse. The violence that children witness (and at times are victims of) in the home or in the media has taken its toll. The FBI reported that of an average 23,000 homicides each year in America, 25 percent of the killers are age twenty-one or less.[11]

Divorce is common and often easily obtained. One in four children (25.5 percent) live in homes with their mothers only—no fathers—according to the U.S. Census Bureau.

> *The appearance of revivals owes nothing to chance;*
> *they are a witness to God's sovereignty.*
>
> James Burns

In spite of all that seems wrong with our country, I believe there are signs indicating we are on the verge of revival. As we discussed in other sections of this book, we see:

- A returning to the centrality of Jesus and the Cross
- A returning to the Bible devotionally for faith and practice
- Explosive witnessing and telling others about Jesus Christ
- A movement of social justice as people begin to obey the Scriptures

Read Isaiah 30. There God gives His Word to the nation that chooses to remain rebellious and obstinate toward God. Name three characteristics of an obstinate nation found in Isaiah 30.

_____

_____

In spite of their rebellion, what was God's desire for Israel?

_____

_____

List three benefits of returning to God as a nation.

_____

_____

Re-read verses 27–33. How do these verses relate to revival?

_____

_____

What are the issues in your world that need an outpouring of God's power?

_____

_____

Pray now for God to move in those situations. Record your prayer.

_____

_____

How do you see God's power converging in your world? What are the signs?

_____

_____

Read Psalm 33:12-22. How is God's power displayed?

_____

_____

REVIEW THE DAY

Read Ezekiel 22:30. How is God calling you to stand in the gap for our country? How can you be a vessel through which God's power can work?

_____

_____

Today make a new commitment to pray for the nation. Write a prayer with that commitment.

_____

_____

What was the most meaningful sentence or Bible verse in this section? Rephrase that particular sentence or verse as a prayer to God.

_____

_____

_____

What action does God want you to take as a result of today's study? Meditate, think deeply, and listen to your heart; then write about the action you will take.

_____

_____

REVIVAL TRUTHS

- While we have many things wrong with our nation, God's power is being displayed.
- God calls us to pray for His power to work in our nation.

KEY VERSE

"So I sought for a man among them who would make a wall, and stand in the gap before Me on behalf of the land, that I should not destroy it; but I found no one". (Ezekiel 22:30 NKJV)

DAY FOUR

UNPARALLELED UNITY AMONG CHRISTIANS

In the United States, God is bringing about a unity within the Christian body as never seen before. While we are united in many ways, I want to focus on three specific aspects of unity. We are united in desperation, united in prayer, and united in desire to seek Him.

American believers are united in desperation—socially, politically, economically, and militarily. We are desperate for leadership. We are desperate because of sin. There is so much sin in our nation that we've redefined sin. More than twenty-five years ago, Karl Menninger, in his classic book, *Whatever Became of Sin* (Hawthorn), showed that when a person has so much sin that he doesn't know what to do with it, he finally redefines it so it's not sin anymore. That has now happened. President Bill Clinton, when talking with Congressmen in 1998, discussed "the fudge factor," a policy in which a leader does not tell the entire truth.[12]

Christian leader and former Washington insider Charles Colson responded to this concept, saying, "It's unimaginable to me that a president of the United States would even suggest that he would lie to avoid carrying out a law that he disagrees with. . . . If we (shrug this off) . . . we would be announcing that we accepted a president who mocks the law."[13]

> *It is not possible to exaggerate the importance of your fellowship with your fellow Christians.*
>
> —◆—
>
> John White

In the midst of this desperation, a movement toward concerted and united prayer among the Christian community has been underway. A national call to prayer issued January 21, 1993, by the National Consultation on United Prayer led the way. Here is what that document said.

The Call

We recognize our absolute dependence on God and our desperate need for divine intervention.

We believe God is urging us to call all Christians of America to unite in humility and repentance across ethnic and church boundaries to pray persistently for a moral and spiritual awakening in the Body of Christ.

We believe this will greatly advance His Kingdom in our nation and worldwide.

The Covenant

We covenant to obey this call by taking the following actions:

- We will promote this call as broadly as possible.
- Individually, we will commune with God and pray with faith daily.
- We will encourage and participate regularly in corporate, believing prayer.
- We will fast as God prompts us.
- Feeling incomplete without embracing God's family from all races, we will seek reconciliation and participation with all our brothers and sisters.
- We will pray until God sovereignly acts.[14]

This call and covenant in January 1993 was developed by three hundred men and women from 166 denominations and ministries. Thirty-five states were represented at this historic gathering. They met initially for twenty-four hours to pray, the purpose of which was to inaugurate a new era of spiritual leadership in the body of Christ, calling the church to united prayer for revival.

The Mission America leadership placed a similar call to prayer in *USA Today* on April 26, 1999. And now, as we begin the third millennium, the Lighthouse Movement has issued an unprecedented call to every believer to be a lighthouse to their neighbors and others within their sphere of influence, beginning with prayer. The goal of each Lighthouse is to pray for, care for, and share the Gospel with every person in the United States.

Have we ever known such boldly unified prayer-evangelism? We are unified in seeking. We are unified in our desire to know Him intimately. We are unified in the early stages of prayer for revival.

Read Matthew 5:6. What does God promise to those who seek Him?

_____

_____

Today we see people hungry for righteousness and with a desire to be filled with God's love like never before. In the history of this nation it is unprecedented for the competitive denominations and parachurch groups to come together in unity to reach out to the nation. For example, the Mission America Coalition is composed of 411 general committee members spanning eighty-four denominations and more than three hundred national parachurch and citywide ministries. The coalition is a network of networks with over seventy national ministry networks involving over three thousand parachurch and citywide leaders. It meets once a year to coordinate these seventy affinity group or ministry function tracks such as prayer, evangelism, men, women, youth, and boys and girls. Together, they desire to reach out with the love of Jesus to every person in this nation.

In Jeremiah 3:3, the Bible discusses God's showers and rain. When God poured out His Spirit at Pentecost in Acts 2, and began to empower the church for the work of the Great Commission, it was the early rain. Today God is pouring out the latter rain. As a farm boy, I knew the early rain came after planting to germinate the seeds. A planted seed is hard and dry, but the rain penetrates the soil to soften and enlarge the seed. Within each seed, the starches change to sugars, and the roots go down. Then shoots go up, and the plant bears fruit. If the latter rain doesn't come, the shoot may come up yet may not become rich for harvest, bearing little or no fruit.

Today we are seeing a special rain, an outpouring of God's Spirit. It softens and breaks the outside kernels of our hearts to produce much fruit and a great harvest. People who have been in the church for years are saying, "I want more out of life. I want to increase my service to God." Like the plants, the insides of people are changing from hard hearts to ones soft toward God.

REVIEW THE DAY

The Lord is bringing people from various parts of the church of Jesus Christ together in a new fashion. How have you experienced this unity in your own life? If you have not experienced this unity, how could you begin to experience it?

Study how Jesus prayed for unity among believers in John 17:20–23. What lessons do you draw for your own life?

Today make a fresh commitment to be a part of God's unity among believers in Jesus. Write a prayer with that commitment below.

What was the most meaningful sentence or Bible verse in this section? Rephrase that particular sentence or verse as a prayer to God.

What action does God want you to take as a result of today's study? Meditate, think deeply, and listen to your heart; then write about the action you will take.

REVIVAL TRUTHS

- There is unprecedented unity among believers in today's church.
- We are especially unified through desperation, prayer, and a desire to seek Him.

 KEY VERSE

And the glory which thou gavest me I have given them; that they may be one, even as we are one: I in them, and thou in me, that they may be made perfect in one; and that the world may know that thou hast sent me, and hast loved them, as thou hast loved me. (John 17:22–23)

DAY FIVE

HOW INDIVIDUAL ACTIONS CAN AFFECT MANY

Once a virtuoso cellist said, "If I miss one day of practice, I know it. If I miss two days, my teacher knows it. If I miss three days, everybody knows it."

I have found this true about my quiet time. If I miss one day, I feel dry that day. If I miss two days, I'm not relating to my wife as I should. If I miss three days, then I begin to be irritated and an irritant. I look at the world differently because I haven't been letting the light of Jesus Christ fill me—through prayer, quiet time, and meditation. My openness to God diminishes; I am less willing to obey His daily call.

As we see God moving in our nation, we must be in continual relationship with Him. We must be devoted to a life of prayer, fasting, Scripture study, and obedience. If we are not, He cannot work through us to bring revival and heal our land. We are the vessels through which God works. Our lives affect others, even those we've never met.

> *My life is in You, Lord,*
> *My strength is in You, Lord,*
> *My hope is in You, Lord,*
> *In You, it's in You.*
>
> ———◄❖►———
>
> "MY LIFE IS IN YOU LORD"/Daniel Gardner

A few years ago, God personally touched a successful university football coach, Bill McCartney. He had a vision to begin a men's movement in the nation and left a big-time program at the University of Colorado to answer God's call. The movement began with a few men coming together to pray and has grown into millions praying, worshipping, and reaching out through an organization called Promise Keepers. Coach McCartney saw a need. He sought God's power through prayer. He became part of the solution to an identified problem.

You can become part of the solution too. Intimacy with Christ will give you the stepping stones to understanding your role. It's between you and Him. Say to God, "I'm just one human being, but what can I do? How can I move into real significance in my relationship with You? How can I let You work through me?"

Stop now and pray. Ask God to show you where you are part of the problem. How can you become part of the solution? Write your response.

_____

_____

Read 2 Corinthians 4:16. Why is renewal on a daily basis so critical?

_____

_____

Do you see even small steps of change as significant? Why or why not?

_____

_____

We begin this journey by being faithful, trusting Him completely. God honors our obedience. If we follow God in every step of our lives, then God will do what He designed for us. Each piece of our life is part of a mosaic that God pieces together for His glory. It's our job to obey; it's God's job to bring results.

REVIEW THE DAY

Do you understand your importance to God? Take a few minutes and meditate on Psalm 139:17–18. What insight and encouragement do you gain from these verses?

_____

_____

_____

Read Proverbs 3:5–6. Are you faithful in following God every day with your life and heart? Write a prayer of affirmation of your faithfulness to God below.

_____

_____

Do you understand the importance of your part in the worldwide plan of God? Write about it below.

_____

_____

Social historian and critic Allan Bloom once wrote about George Washington:

[His] life reflect[ed] his profound faith in God. . . . He directed his men to be punctual in attendance for worship services and to refrain from cursing. He realized that God was not likely to grant victory to an army that profaned His name. . . . In his own hand, Washington wrote, "Direct my thoughts, words, and work, wash away my sins in the immaculate Blood of the Lamb, and purge my heart by Thy Holy Spirit. . . . Daily frame me more and more into the likeness of Thy Son, Jesus Christ."[15]

What can we learn from George Washington's example? Do you ask God to direct your thoughts, your words, and your work? Do you ask God to wash away your sins? Do you ask God to frame your day to be more like Jesus Christ? Write such a prayer below.

_____

_____

What was the most meaningful sentence or Bible verse in this section? Rephrase that particular sentence or verse as a prayer to God.

_____

_____

_____

_____

What action does God want you to take as a result of today's study? Meditate, think deeply, and listen to your heart; then write about the action you will take.

_____

_____

REVIVAL TRUTHS

- Our lives affect others, even those we don't know.
- We are to live faithful lives in relationship with Christ.
- God wants to use us in His plan.
- Our response is to be faithful and obedient to God's daily call.

KEY VERSE

How precious also are thy thoughts unto me, O God! how great is the sum of them! (Psalm 139:17)

LOOKING AHEAD

As we grow personally and reach out to others, we have the potential to impact our entire nation with the Gospel of Christ. But our impact extends beyond that. As we shall see, we can also impact the world.

11 VISION FOR THE WORLD

The world is a big place, and the concept of touching more than two hundred nations for Christ sounds overwhelming. Yet throughout Scripture we are told to proclaim His truth throughout the world, to every person.

"Declare His glory among the nations, His wonders among all peoples. Let the heavens rejoice, and let the earth be glad; and let them say among the nations, 'The Lord reigns.'" (1 Chronicles 16:24, 31 NKJV)

"Declare His glory among the nations, His wonders among all peoples" (Psalm 96:3 NKJV).

"O give thanks unto the Lord; call upon his name: make known his deeds among the people" (Psalm 105:1).

How we view the world can make all the difference. Do we see it as a world created and owned by God, full of people who don't know they're called to be His children? Do we see the world as one family divided by sin? Or do we see differences in skin color, cultures, and lifestyles that cause us to hesitate in accepting our part in reaching the world for Christ? Let's consider our worldview, and how we can touch and love the world for Christ.

DAY ONE

THIS IS MY FATHER'S WORLD

In the beginning, there was nothing, Genesis 1:2. Everything was without form and void. We learn that God *bara*—made out of nothing—the world. The world came from the heart of God. Why? Because He's a creative God, and He wanted a place for His creation. The planet is for those who would be in fellowship with Him. Unlike angels, who are obliged to have fellowship with the Lord, mankind was created to choose fellowship with the Father. God wanted something to love, so He spoke man into being. The world is a part of God's creation and was made perfect. By giving humans a free will, creation was marked with the potential for imperfection. Mankind couldn't be perfect if the potential for imperfection didn't exist.

God created us for fellowship, love, and worship. Revelation 4–5, 7:9–17 describes the activities of heaven—God being honored, praised, and worshipped. Part of the spiritual fall on earth was the separation of our "belongings" from us. Now we have to earn what was already ours—which takes an enormous amount of time and energy from our life. Our purpose for existence was clouded. Initially we were created for fellowship with God, but now we often seek work as a reason for living. We miss the greatest activity possible—to love God. Revival is about this process of returning to the reason for our existence.

People ask questions like, "Why am I here? What's my purpose? What's the reason for my being?" The answers were clear before the Fall. Now they have to be sought and found. We must *choose* to return to God. Our God is jealous; He wants people who are made in His image to love Him out of their own desire.

How do you view the world you live in? Do you consider it at all?

Do you see God as the Creator of all? Why or why not?

_____

_____

When I was twelve years old, Mom drove me to downtown Corinth, Mississippi for shopping. We covered those seven miles from our farm in Kossuth in a 1951 green Studebaker, and on the way I thought about the story I had heard in Sunday school the week before. My teacher, Gerald Wegman, a mechanic, had helped the children study the Tower of Babel story. I found the story intriguing. If God made the world and everything in it, why was this tower so perverse? The story made it clear that though mankind was united, they left out the need for God. Instead of giving God the glory, they were going to build a tall tower to get as high as possible —to be like God. The Lord looked down and gave them different languages so they couldn't communicate to finish the tower.

> *For the beauty of the earth,*
> *For the glory of the skies . . .*
> *Lord of all, to Thee we raise*
> *This our hymn of grateful praise.*
>
> ———◆———
>
> "FOR THE BEAUTY OF THE EARTH"/Folliott S. Pierpoint

As I rode with my mother, I reflected on what had happened since then: People have not lived together in harmony and don't speak the same language. Suddenly I thought, *Wow, look at the United States! It's a nation that came together to seek Jesus Christ for freedom to worship God without the force of a state religion. And the whole world lives here with immigrants from every country of the world. And essentially the U.S. uses the same language.*

"Mom, is it possible that the United States of America is an experiment by God to reverse the Tower of Babel and see if we as a nation can live together and love each other under Jesus Christ? Is it possible?"

My mom was taken back by the question. She said, "Son, I don't know. That's an interesting thought."

In my heart, I began to understand the special nature of this country. The United States is special not because the people or the government or the land is special in itself, but because of God. Even on our coinage, the words are printed, "In God We Trust."

It is possible as a nation to live together in harmony. But each of us must work to bring about truth as an objective anchor from which we can work to develop the best relationship possible with each other and the Lord.

Today Christ is the unifying factor in our spiritual life. English is the predominate world language. Could the United States be the cap on the dynamite stick to bring about a worldwide return to Him? We should pray to that end.

REVIEW THE DAY

Read Acts 17:26–27. Consider for a few minutes your larger purpose in the world. Why did God create you? What is your purpose? Write some thoughts about this question in the space below.

_____

_____

Read the account of the Tower of Babel in Genesis 11:1–9. How does the United States compare with this period from Bible history? What do you think about the concept of America being of one language and a miniature picture of the world in one place?

_____

_____

What steps can you take to increase your awareness of the world spiritually?

_____

_____

Today make a commitment to learn more about the world and increase your awareness of what is happening in our world and culture. Write a prayer with that commitment below.

_____

_____

_____

What was the most meaningful sentence or Bible verse in this section? Rephrase that particular sentence or verse as a prayer to God.

_____

_____

_____

_____

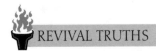

REVIVAL TRUTHS

- The world was created by God for His pleasure.
- We were created to be in fellowship with God.
- We are a part of the world as individuals, and as a country.

KEY VERSE

He has made from one blood every nation of men to dwell on all the face of the earth, and has determined their preappointed times and the boundaries of their dwellings, so that they should seek the Lord, in the hope that they might grope for Him and find Him, though He is not far from each one of us. (Acts 17:26–27 NKJV)

DAY TWO

MY VISION
OF THE WORLD

What is your vision for the world? Is it a big place or small? Do you see the world as a place God made and is trying to bring back to Himself? Or do you see the world as two-hundred-plus nations and thousands of people groups who can't live in harmony?

Do you see the world as full of children whom God loves and about whom He cares equally? Or is your vision more narrow and you believe one group is better than another? Do you see the world as having the potential of being unified? Is that good or bad?

How do you view the world? Ultimately, is the world God's, or is it man's? Or is it Satan's? Do you regard God as the creator and sustainer of all? Your beliefs about the world impact what you think about God and yourself.

How do you view the world? Is it a good place or bad place?

_____

_____

Are we related to each other biologically or even as part of God's family?

_____

_____

Why does your world view matter?

_____

_____

Do you care about the other countries and people groups in the world? Do you see that as part of your place in the kingdom of God?

_____

_____

Read Matthew 23:37. Jesus was grieving for His own city; He loved His people and desired that they would know the truth of God. That is very clear. Now read Matthew 28:19–20. In these verses we also see that Jesus' heart is for the entire world. There is a time and place to be focused on home, and there is also a time and place to focus outside of our country into the world. God is the God of the entire world, not just the United States.

From 1997–2000, International Students, Inc., has been holding evangelistic and discipleship conferences for mainland Chinese students and scholars. Through these events we have seen many come to know Christ for the first time, others baptized, and others make commitments of full-time service in China for Christ—to take the truth of Jesus Christ and His salvation to China.

> ### *Revival is . . .*
> *the inrush of divine life into a body*
> *threatening to become a corpse.*
>
> ———◆———
>
> D.M. Panton

One of the greatest blessings is to hear the testimonies of those students and scholars who have felt God's call to return to China as indigenous (or native) missionaries. They leave profitable careers in the United States in fields of science, medicine, technology, and education to serve God in China. The Great Commission fuels their fire. Many feel that China will become the largest missionary-sending country in the world, and they want to be a part of it. Their burden is not just for China, but for the world.

When we look at the world through spiritual eyes, we should be able to visualize, as the prophet Ezekiel did, a valley of dry bones. Spiritually the world is dry, and God wants to raise these bones to life. First, God moves the church in revival, then among the unconverted, awakening them to their lost condition and the hope of salvation through Jesus Christ. Dry bones can live!

REVIEW THE DAY

Read Ezekiel 37:1–14. Look at this prophecy related to the dry bones. What is God saying through this image to you today about His work in the world? Write your insight below.

_____

_____

Read Matthew 28:18–20. What type of authority has Jesus been given and as a result has given to us? Note that these words of Jesus aren't written as a request but a command. What are you doing to increase your vision for the world based on the Great Commission?

_____

_____

Consider your own vision for reaching the world for Christ. Do you have a vision? Can you verbalize it in the space below?

_____

_____

Today make a fresh commitment for God to use you in reaching the world for Jesus. Write a prayer with that commitment below.

_____

_____

What was the most meaningful sentence or Bible verse in this section? Rephrase that particular sentence or verse as a prayer to God.

_____

_____

VISION FOR THE WORLD

What action does God want you to take as a result of today's study? Meditate, think deeply, and listen to your heart; then write about the action you will take.

_____

_____

REVIVAL TRUTHS

- Our vision for the world should mirror what God wants for the world.
- God's desire is for all people to know His truth.

KEY VERSE

And shall put my spirit in you, and ye shall live, and I shall place you in your own land: then shall ye know that I the Lord have spoken it, and performed it, saith the Lord. (Ezekiel 37:14)

DAY THREE

MY PLACE
IN THE WORLD

Your whole world begins with you. Your world does not begin with your spouse, or your children, or your best friends. It doesn't begin with your neighborhood or with your pastor or your church. It doesn't begin with the leaders of your community, city, state, or nation. Your world begins with you.

Is there anybody who impacts your world more than you? No and yes. No—if you are not totally surrendered to Jesus Christ, and you are not intimate with Him. Yes—if you have an intimacy with Christ, and you give yourself to Him every day as Lord. In that case, your world is impacted by God through you.

For example, if I am a free man, no one impacts my world more than me. But if I'm a slave and have an owner, who impacts my world more—the slave or the owner? The owner.

Who owns your life? Whoever owns your life will impact your world the most. Do you own your life? Or does Christ own your life?

Read Romans 8:7–9. How does this verse relate to ownership in your life?

_____

_____

If you own your life, then your focus will be to impact the world for yourself. If Christ owns your life, then your life will have two desires for impact—first for Him, and then for others. Interestingly, God always cares for our needs in the process of serving Him and others. To reach our world for Christ, our focus must be on others—not on ourselves.

Take a moment and pray. Ask God to show you areas where you are self-centered rather than others-centered. Record His response.

_____

_____

How do you become others-centered? Let's consider the concept of slavery. Read 1 Peter 2:9, which describes followers of God as a "chosen generation . . . His own special people" (NKJV). Do you belong to God? If you belong to God, how can you set your own agenda? When we read God's Word, we can determine the Lord's agenda.

Read Hebrews 12:5–6. Is God dealing with you? Are you going to respond to Him? Or is the greatest motivation in your life personal? Who is directing your life? You or God? Record your thoughts.

_____

_____

Read Mark 8:34–35. Every person innately wants to save his or her own life in a sense and make his or her own decisions. Each of us must deal with the independent, me-first attitude. Have you noticed how individualism is a key philosophy in America? For example, we don't prefer mass transit; one person per car is the typical morning commute. Frank Sinatra, the gifted and independent-minded singer, made his anthem, "I did it my way." Of course, there is no question that each of us is an individual; yet our culture has taken this individualization to extreme. There is no meaning in life outside of "my box." If you learn to handle only what is inside your box or realm of influence, you miss God's call to be part of a greater plan.

Our place in this world is to be part of the body of Christ. That body is located across the world, not just within our individual churches, or even the United States. Scripture says that when one part of the body weeps, we all weep. When one part rejoices, we all rejoice.

Do you weep with persecuted believers across the world? Do you see them as part of the same body? Why or why not?

_____

_____

> ### Revival is . . .
> *always the action of God. It is not man.*
> *It is God pouring out His Spirit.*
>
> ————◆◆◆————
>
> D.M. Lloyd-Jones

Jesus gives us the command to turn and seek God, saying in Matthew 6:33, "But seek ye first the kingdom of God, and his righteousness; and all these things shall be added unto you." In our culture, we have internally paraphrased this verse to become, "I'll seek my way first and if I can get to my end." In marriage and family life, this individual bent has had its toll on our children. As syndicated columnist Cal Thomas wrote, "Too many parents are divorcing. . . . Too many children think they are unwanted and unloved, that they disturb our comfort, rob us of pleasure, and cost us money, which we regretfully spend on them."[1] It's all *my* desire and *my* own way.

To have the greatest return on our existence, we as a nation must seek God's will. As we follow God's principles, we will experience the greatest blessings of life. Hebrews 11:27 declares, "By faith he [Moses] . . . endured, as seeing him who is invisible." Notice the element of faith in Moses, and it's the same for us. Faith carries us like nothing else. Even though our faith is invisible, if we trust God, we will have the result that we want in our lives—fulfillment and joy—as each of us finds the place He has created just for you, just for me.

The apostle Peter wrote, "Arm yourselves also with the same mind, . . . that he no longer should live the rest of his time in the flesh for the lusts of men, but for the will of God" (1 Peter 4:1–2 NKJV). What is our motive—to do our thing or the will of God? Is our attitude to put on self or to put on Christ?

If our foundation is self, there is no power. We will be making our way by ourselves, often at the expense of others. If our foundation is in Christ, there is power. The Bible tells us in Romans 6:19 that we are weak in our natural self. John 3:6 says, "That which is born of the flesh is flesh; and that which is born of the Spirit is spirit."

REVIEW THE DAY

Every day when you get up, are you stepping out in the flesh or by faith stepping out in the power of God's Spirit? Write an honest answer in the space below.

_____

_____

Take a few minutes and examine the foundation of your life. Is it rooted in self or the Savior? What fills your daily thoughts and life (see 1 Corinthians 3:11)?

_____

_____

What steps can you take to increase your thoughts about the Lord and begin to reach the world around you?

_____

_____

Today make a new commitment for the Lord to be the foundation of your life and give you new ideas to reach the world for Jesus. Write a prayer with that commitment below.

_____

_____

What was the most meaningful sentence or Bible verse in this section? Rephrase that particular sentence or verse as a prayer to God.

_____

_____

_____

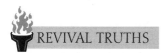

REVIVAL TRUTHS

- God has created a special place for me in the world.
- I am called to a selfless, rather than a selfish life.
- I am connected to all believers in the body of Christ throughout the world.

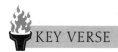

KEY VERSE

Now when He was asked by the Pharisees when the kingdom of God would come, He answered them and said, "The kingdom of God does not come with observation; nor will they say, 'See here!' or 'See there!' For indeed, the kingdom of God is within you." (Luke 17:20–21 NKJV)

DAY FOUR

THE WORLD
AT YOUR DOOR

In 1988, Benazir Bhutto became the first woman to lead a Muslim nation in modern times. Before Benazir went to college at Harvard-Radcliffe, her father, Pakistan's Prime Minister Zufikar Al Bhutto, gave her a beautiful copy of the Qu'ran. He told her, "You will see many things that surprise you in America, and some that may shock you. But I know you have the ability to adapt. Above all you must study hard. Very few in Pakistan have the opportunity you now have, and you must take advantage of it. Never forget that the money it is costing to send you comes from the land, from the people who sweat and toil on those lands. You will owe a debt to them, a debt you can repay with God's blessing by using your education to better their lives."[2]

Benazir's first encounter with American students at Radcliffe was an eye-opener. She wrote about those early college days in her biography, *Daughter of Destiny*:

> "Pak-i-stan? Where's Pak-i-stan?" my new classmates asked me when I first arrived at Radcliffe.
>
> "Pakistan is the largest Muslim country in the world," I replied, sounding like a handout from our embassy. "There are two wings of Pakistan separated by India."
>
> "Oh, India," came the relieved response. "You're next to India."
>
> I smarted every time I heard the reference to India, with whom we had had two bitter wars. Pakistan was supposed to be one of America's strongest allies. . . . The United States used our air bases in northern Pakistan for their U-2 reconnaissance flights including the ill-fated flight of Gary Powers in 1960. . . . Yet Americans seemed completely unaware even of the existence of my country.[3]

Today, Benazir Bhutto takes her experiences from the land of Harvard into her everyday decisions and actions as she leads this Muslim nation.

What if Bhutto had met loving Christians while here in the United States? What if she went home not just with an education, but with Jesus?

Over 600,000 international students are studying in the United States right now, representing almost every part of the world. They are the best and brightest their countries have to offer. In five to twenty years, many will be the leaders of their nations. Other international students will return home and eventually have a powerful influence over the industry, education, economics, science, politics, technology, agriculture, and faith of their countries. They will return home to make a difference. The question is, "Will they make a difference for Jesus Christ?"

> *In revival the Church returns to the glory and power that prevailed at Pentecost.*
>
> J. Edwin Orr

Admittedly the world is a huge place. In the United States alone are more than 270 million people, and the world has a population of over six billion. It's easy to be overwhelmed by these numbers. Instead of feeling insignificant, let's consider the possibilities. "Every soul is equally precious in God's sight, but not every soul is equally strategic," as Campus Crusade's Bill Bright notes. Every individual who does not have a personal relationship with Jesus Christ is lost and bound for an eternity separated from God. This is critical to God. However, some who come to know Christ carry more influence to effect change in others around them. These international students are strategic.

While they come to America with specific educational goals and plans, most of them are unaware of a personal divine plan from God. Immersed into a new culture and away from family and friends, these international students are often lonely. They feel out of place, lost, and anxious about understanding new people and new situations. Simple tasks can be bewildering for the international student—such as how to locate housing, or banking, or the difference between a grocery store, drug store, specialty shop, and a department store. As caring and committed Christians cross their paths and offer friendship in Him, international students learn about the greatest friend of all—Jesus Christ.

Several years ago, one of our staff attended a college president's reception for incoming international students at a California university. The president asked two graduating seniors to tell about their experiences in the U.S. during the last few years.

A Middle Eastern student stood stiffly behind the podium and began. "I have been in America for four years, and these have been the most lonely years of my life. When I walk down a hallway and an American says with a smile, 'Hi, how are you doing?' I stop and try to tell them how I am doing. Instead they just keep on walking and don't really care about my answer."

Our history at International Students indicates this student's story is all too common. Statistics prove that among the international students who study in the U.S., historically 70 percent have never been invited inside an American home. More than 80 percent are never invited to an American church nor have any meaningful contact with genuine Christians during an average stay of four years. These students have a tremendous need for personal relationships. They are open to anyone who will stretch out their hand and say, "I'll be your friend." We can change these statistics—one lonely student at a time. Each of us can be that friend. Through your friendship with an international, you can expand your view of the world and potentially have a profound impact for God's kingdom.

We can start by praying for the international students and scholars near us.

REVIEW THE DAY

Read Acts 8:26–40 about Phillip and the Ethiopian eunuch. Note how with boldness yet in the power of the Spirit, Phillip witnessed to this international leader. What insight do you gain about your own witnessing from this illustration?

_____

_____

Read Acts 1:8 and think about your own life and circle of friends. What are you doing to reach Jerusalem (your own neighborhood), Samaria (the region), and the ends of the earth? Make some definite plans below and also write a brief prayer for God to use your life for the world.

_____

_____

_____

_____

Read Genesis 21:23, Exodus 22:21, and Leviticus 19:33. How are we to treat aliens living among us?

_____

_____

Do you live near a college or university? Have you considered reaching out to the international students on that campus? Why or why not?

_____

_____

Can you commit to pray for international students? Write that commitment.

_____

_____

What was the most meaningful sentence or Bible verse in this section? Rephrase that particular sentence or verse as a prayer to God.

_____

_____

_____

 REVIVAL TRUTHS

- Through international leaders who are studying in our country, the world is at our door.
- We can commit to pray for these students, and we can commit to reach them through friendship on a campus near our homes.
- These leaders will go home to influence their country and the world, but will they do it with Jesus?

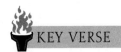
KEY VERSE

But ye shall receive power, after that the Holy Ghost is come upon you: and ye shall be witnesses unto me both in Jerusalem, and in all Judaea, and in Samaria, and unto the uttermost part of the earth. (Acts 1:8)

DAY FIVE

IMPACT THE
WORLD FOR ETERNITY

Charlie Riggs was an oil field roustabout from New York and Pennsylvania who came to Christ in his teens. His dad left home when he was a little boy, so Charlie had to begin working at age five to help support his family. As a teenager, he worked in a bowling alley setting pins. Charlie never got to finish college because he became an officer in the military. He joined a Bible study with the Navigator ministry that began to do the follow-up for Billy Graham's crusades.

Later the Navigators opened their ministry in Seattle, and Dawson Trotman, the Navigators founder, called Lorne Sanny, who was leading a Bible study with Charlie. Dawson asked, "How is the Bible study going?" Lorne was quiet.

"How many do you have attending?" Dawson asked.

"I just have one."

"What's his name?" Dawson asked.

"Lieutenant Charles Riggs."

"Is he faithful?"

"Oh, he's faithful."

After a pause, Trotman said, "Well, Lorne, I think you should major on Riggs."[4]

The Bible says, "A faithful man who can find?" (Proverbs 20:6). If you are faithful, then God will use you. Charlie Riggs went on to serve in the Billy Graham Evangelistic Association as the director of follow-up and counseling for forty years, doing an incredible job throughout the world. Most people are not faithful. Why is Billy Graham, the farm boy from North Carolina, "Billy Graham," the steady, consistent evangelist for five decades? It's his faithfulness.

There are two kinds of vision; one is external and the other is internal. External vision looks at the world and follows the seemingly obvious progressive stages of

VISION FOR THE WORLD

life offered. Many of those external stages are from true principles, such as if you work hard, you get a return. Or if you help people, they will probably help you.

A vision for the world involves internal sight and wisdom. Jesus said in Matthew 11:19, "But wisdom is justified of her children." Internal wisdom sees the sin and corruption of the world and weeps for the deception under which people live. Internal wisdom realizes that this world is not our home, but that eternity is. By having internal wisdom we invest our time, talents, treasure, and testimony for God's world and not our own.

> *How lovely on the mountains are the feet of him*
> *who brings good news, good news:*
> *Announcing peace, proclaiming news of happiness,*
> *Our God reigns. Our God reigns!*
>
> "OUR GOD REIGNS"/Leonard E. Smith

Can you say, "God, by faith I am going to follow your leading and Your Word today and believe that wisdom is proved by her actions? Help me to live in the real world but to also see the real, real world—that world that never dies, where the investment of my life in every way will bring the greatest return."

The Bible tells us that wisdom is (1) from above, (2) peaceable, and (3) easy to be entreated (James 3:17). Will we let wisdom guide us as we look at our world?

Do you have an external view of the world, or an internal? What do your actions show?

_____

_____

We can't address the needs of the world or the workplace unless we are filled to overflowing with God's spirit love. Consider and pray through the apostle Paul's prayer for the Philippians. It can be our heart cry as well. "And this I pray, that your love may abound yet more and more in knowledge and in all judgment; that ye may approve things that are excellent; that ye may be sincere and without offence till the day of Christ; being filled with the fruits of righteousness, which are by Jesus Christ, unto the glory and praise of God" (Philippians 1:9–11).

REVIEW THE DAY

Do you have this internal sight from God? Do you believe God enough to know that you were made for a purpose? If you are obedient, disciplined, and intimate with God, then God will guide you into your life purpose.

Read Proverbs 9. What is the difference between wisdom and folly?

_____

_____

What are the benefits of wisdom?

_____

_____

How does wisdom relate to our ability to impact the world?

_____

_____

Evaluate your internal sight and God's purpose for your life in the space below.

_____

_____

Do you believe that you are a part of the mosaic of God's work around the world? Do you believe that God has created a place for you? Briefly, write what you know about God's purpose at this point in your life in the space below.

_____

_____

Use the following prayer to commit your life to God's purposes:

"Lord, help me to have internal sight. Help me not to be simply guided by what I see but what I believe. While I live in a real world, help me to daily, moment by moment, see the real, real world—that world that never deteriorates and is steadfast —Your world. Give me wisdom from above that is pure and easy to be molded to Your will. Lead me to fit into Your big picture for my life. God, day by day shape me into the person You want me to become."

Make a commitment to be faithful to God's wisdom and call in your life. Write that commitment.

_____

_____

What was the most meaningful sentence or Bible verse in this section? Rephrase that particular sentence or verse as a prayer to God.

_____

_____

_____

REVIVAL TRUTHS

- Inner sight comes from God's hand.
- We can choose to live according to the world's external view, or God's internal view.
- Faithfulness is required.

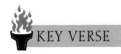

KEY VERSE

Most men will proclaim every one his own goodness: but a faithful man who can find? (Proverbs 20:6)

LOOKING AHEAD

The world is a big place, but it begins in exactly one spot—you. Having a world view based on God's perspective is important. Sometimes we leave our country to reach the world, but we can also reach the world at home through international students. In our final chapter we will put together those pieces and others in the book to see revival happen moment by moment, day by day.

12 OUR RESPONSE— ONE DAY AT A TIME

How do you become a person who knows the Bible? You memorize one verse at a time.

How do you become a person with many friends? You build your relationships one person at a time.

How do you get to be a good husband or wife or a good son or daughter? You find the needs of another person and then try to meet those needs one at a time.

How do you live life? Whether you like it or not, it's one day at a time. One hour at a time. One moment at a time.

How do you build depth with Jesus Christ? You get to know Him by spending one minute at a time with Him.

How does revival begin? With one changed heart at a time.

A key question for each of us to ask is, "Is what I'm doing today that which will help to accomplish the results that I intend for my life?" More importantly, we should ask, "Will it accomplish God's will for my life?" What results do you want in your life? Your goals? God's direction?

Every day you need to ask yourself this key question. "Of all I could do, which will contribute most to that which I am called to accomplish?"

DAY ONE

DAILY VISION

Where are your eyes focused? Perhaps they're focused on yourself, perhaps on your job, or perhaps on your family. In spite of all the important relationships in our lives, we are called to focus our eyes on only one place: Jesus Christ. With our eyes focused on Him, we'll receive all that we require to carry out what He has placed before us. This requires a daily refocusing of our vision, a daily realignment of our spiritual eyes.

We are faced with thousands of choices each day. Choices about how we think, what we wear, who we talk to. Some decisions appear small and insignificant, while others may be life-changing. What we often fail to realize is that every single decision builds on another. Even the smallest choices impact our lives.

Read Luke 19:11–17. In the beginning of this parable, Jesus teaches that if we are faithful in the small things of life, we can be trusted for more important work.

In chapter 9 I mentioned the bold witness of Cassie Bernall, the Columbine High School student who died after answering yes about her relationship with Jesus Christ. She had previously rebelled against faith in her life, but came to make Jesus the center of her being day by day. Her life is an example of small decisions that add up to impact a life—like being consistent in attending a church youth group. Her parents noted in an open letter to the community in the newspaper on May 1, 1999:

> Cassie's response does not surprise us. Her life was rightly centered around our Lord Jesus. It was for her strong faith in God and His promise of eternal life that she made her stand. It is clear to me that this tragic incident has been thrown back into the face of Satan and his followers with an impact that is much greater than what was intended for us, God's children.

275

To all young people who hear this, don't let my daughter's death be for nothing. Make your stand. If you're not in the local church's youth group, try it. They want you and will help support you in doing what is right. It's not easy, you'll need one another.[1]

They concluded their letter with this reminder to parents: "We are the front line in all issues regarding our children. Yes, Jesus is the author and finisher of our faith. He is the One that we give our lives to, desire to be like, want to be intimate with, and desire to make known. By following His example, we can see and should see our nation changed, one person at a time."

> *The sense in which a Christian leaves it to God is that he puts all his trust in Christ: trust that Christ will somehow share with him the perfect human obedience which He carried out from His birth to His crucifixion.*
>
> C.S. Lewis

If Cassie had not been making daily decisions with her eyes focused on Christ, would she have been able to respond affirmatively about her relationship with Christ in the face of death? She may have been murdered regardless of her response, but what a testimony she left because of her daily faithfulness.

Where are your eyes focused? Why?

_____

_____

Is this where God would have you look?

_____

_____

We can also turn our eyes toward other people, which leads to envy. Read 1 Samuel 18:6–11. Saul had been the anointed ruler of Israel, yet he heard the great acclaim being given to David. Saul began paying attention to what David was doing rather than on the calling of God for his own life. Because Saul's eyes were focused on David, Saul had opened the door for envy, which would lead to anger and fear. Earlier Saul had prophesied in God's strength (10:10–13); now he attempted to murder David. How did this happen? Saul's vision was clouded by not focusing on God.

One of the daily choices I face is how I see myself compared to how God sees me. The more I grow in my relationship with Christ, the more I realize how inadequate I am. Such a perspective can be healthy; however, I can focus so much on my inadequacies that I take my eyes off Jesus. An inverted pride takes over that keeps me absorbed with myself. Each day I must decide where I will focus. Will it be on Jesus, who makes me complete? Or will it be on myself? It's an important choice, one each of us must make.

Read 2 Corinthians 3:4–6. Why is it important to keep our eyes on Jesus when we consider our worth?

_____

_____

Do you know the freedom of relying on Christ daily, seeking Him daily? Explain your answer.

_____

_____

REVIEW THE DAY

If we focus on anything but Christ, we are unable to see clearly. Our vision is clouded with the cares of the world, rather than the peace of God.

Read Hebrews 12:2. How can you have joy in the midst of the trials of life?

_____

_____

Ask God to show you what blocks your view of Christ. Write His response.

_____

_____

What was the most meaningful sentence or Bible verse in this section? Rephrase that particular sentence or verse as a prayer to God.

_____

_____

What action does God want you to take as a result of today's study? Meditate, think deeply, and listen to your heart; then write about the action you will take.

_____

_____

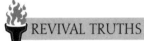

REVIVAL TRUTHS

- We need to daily focus on Christ to lead us.
- We have choices that may be small or large, but all are important.
- If we are faithful in the small things, God will honor us.
- If we focus on ourselves, we cannot see Christ.

KEY VERSE

Looking unto Jesus the author and finisher of our faith; who for the joy that was set before him endured the cross, despising the shame, and is set down at the right hand of the throne of God. (Hebrews 12:2)

DAY TWO

DAILY
BATTLE

Abraham Lincoln once said something to the effect that the only common ground between good and evil is the battleground. Spiritual warfare is a daily battle. Are you willing to walk in spiritual warfare every day? Some days may be easy and some days may be hard. Are you willing to battle for Jesus?

Yes, we are in a battle, and God guides us in knowing how to win the spiritual warfare. Psychologist Carl Jung said that one must be positively blind not to see the colossal role that evil plays in the world. It has required the intervention of God Himself to deliver humanity from the curse of evil; without His intervention men would remain lost.

We are all on Satan's hit list. From the time of Adam and Eve, when they willfully disobeyed God, the battle for our spirits has been part of life. But though the battle rages around us, the enemy is not flesh and blood.

Read Ephesians 6:12. Who do we battle against?

_____

_____

Though the battle is spiritual, our enemy doesn't usually show up wearing horns and a tail. That would be too obvious. Instead, he comes to us as he did to Eve in the garden, offering what is pleasing to our human ears and eyes. But beware, he is not our friend.

OUR RESPONSE—ONE DAY AT A TIME

Read Matthew 10:16 and John 10:10. Summarize the meaning of those verses for your life.

_____

_____

How does the enemy steal from you? Perhaps you have never considered this question, but think about it. Does he steal your time from God? That can easily happen. Sometimes we may spend time watching television when God has called us to another activity. That's time we have stolen.

Does the enemy steal your purity? We don't need to watch pornographic movies to lose our pure thoughts. We can read magazines that are filled with gossip about the private lives of famous people. That contaminates a mind from being renewed in Christ. Does the enemy destroy your innocence? When we allow him to expose us to movies or books that contain material unnecessary for us to know about, or to vocabulary we would never hear otherwise, our innocence can disappear. I heard a preacher once say that he was amazed at how people would pay money to have someone swear at them. It's destructive.

Where does the enemy steal from you?

_____

_____

Do you realize that he is doing that? If so, why do you allow it? If not, can you recognize that now?

_____

_____

I'm not suggesting that we live with our heads in the sand. But if we could open ourselves to be more sensitive to the Holy Spirit and His work in our lives, we would make different choices.

God has given us the tools to fight the spiritual battle:

- armor (Ephesians 6)
- every spiritual blessing in Christ (Ephesians 1:3)
- the authority of His Name (Philippians 2:10)
- the power in His blood that gives us access to God (Hebrews 10:19–20)
- confidence in knowing that God has already won the battle (Romans 8:31–39).

280

> *There is power, power,*
> *Wonder working power*
> *In the precious blood of the Lamb.*
>
> ———◆———
>
> "THERE IS POWER IN THE BLOOD"/Lewis E. Jones

While spiritual warfare is not the primary topic of this book, I would encourage you to read further. C. Peter Wagner has written several books on the topic of intercession and spiritual warfare (see two of them on the resource page at the back of this book). We need to keep our eyes on Christ, but let us not be ignorant of the battle at hand.

Read Matthew 10:16. Why is it important to not be ignorant of the spiritual battle at hand? Make a commitment now to be wiser.

_____

_____

Are you willing and ready to resist all the enemy offers? It takes discipline. It takes courage. But God has already won the war. We just need to stay in the battle.

REVIEW THE DAY

Where is your battle the most fierce?

_____

_____

Pray now and ask God to give you the courage to fight, knowing He is already victorious.

_____

_____

OUR RESPONSE—ONE DAY AT A TIME

What was the most meaningful sentence or Bible verse in this section? Rephrase that particular sentence or verse as a prayer to God.

_____

_____

_____

_____

What action does God want you to take as a result of today's study? Meditate, think deeply, and listen to your heart; then write about the action you will take.

_____

_____

REVIVAL TRUTHS

- Our battle is spiritual, not against flesh and blood.
- The enemy wants to steal and kill and destroy us.
- We must daily choose to live according to God and not give in to the enemy.

KEY VERSE

For we wrestle not against flesh and blood, but against principalities, against powers, against the rulers of the darkness of this world, against spiritual wickedness in high places. (Ephesians 6:12)

DAY THREE

DAILY
VICTORY

Earlier in this book I described having a spiritual plumb bob; I mentioned that I use Ephesians 6:10–18 daily to help keep me in alignment with God. Take a moment and reread those verses on the armor of God. I realize that they are familiar, but I firmly believe they're a key to daily victory. Spiritual armor is not something extra special we utilize only when the going gets tough, but rather it is necessary clothing for our daily battle.

Imagine getting up in the morning and having a cup of coffee while you read the newspaper. It's a nice day, sunny and warm outside. You're looking forward to a day of strolling through the park with a close friend. Nothing stressful awaits you. It's a glorious and perfect morning. After your coffee you jump in the shower . . . nice and hot. You feel clean after washing off the dirt that bodies collect each day. You've covered yourself with fragrant soaps and shampoos. (Even if you're a guy, it's OK to enjoy being clean and smelling good!)

You leave the shower refreshed and revived. Then you dry off, comb your hair, maybe even dry it and style it. If you're a woman, you may add some make-up. You're all ready for a new day, right? Well, I wouldn't recommend stepping too far out of the house just yet—you're still naked.

Yet that's how we most often face the day. Naked. Unclothed in the armor that God has provided. We may confess our sin and be cleansed in God's forgiveness. We may even put on the fragrance of God's Word. But we're still not clothed—not ready for the day. Do you want daily victory in Christ? Start by dressing for the occasion.

Do you put on spiritual armor daily? Why or why not?

_____

_____

Make a commitment to dress in armor for ten days in a row. Record your start date. Then come back to this page and record the differences you've noticed in your ability to have daily victory.

_____

_____

My spiritual mentor, Charlie Riggs, wrote a book entitled *Learning to Walk with God*. It's an excellent book for helping Christians see God as more real in their lives. Charlie described spiritual warfare and tools for victory. It's important to not only be dressed properly, but to carry the right weapons. Let's consider the five weapons Charlie discussed.[2]

> *A good soldier will become well-acquainted with his weapons because he needs them in the battle.*
>
> —◆—
>
> Charlie Riggs

1. *Rely on Jesus Christ as your advocate.* Realize that God is a sovereign God, and that Jesus Christ is our advocate. Read 1 John 2:1–2, 1 Corinthians 10:13, and James 4:7. How do those apply in your daily battle?

_____

_____

2. *Rely on the Word of God.* Riggs noted that when Jesus was tempted in Luke 4:1–13, He utilized Scripture to battle Satan. We've talked about the importance of spending time in the Word, so at this point I'll say, "Just do it!" Read Psalm 119:9, 11; Hebrews 4:12; and 1 John 2:14. Why is the Word of God so vital?

_____

_____

3. *Pray . . . pray . . . pray.* I've emphasized that throughout this book. Read Matthew 26:41 and write how you will apply prayer to your daily battle for victory:

_____

_____

4. *Submit to the Holy Spirit.* Each of us has been created to be a body that submits to a soul, a soul that submits to a spirit, and a spirit that submits to God's Spirit. Read 1 Thessalonians 5:23. Are you in alignment with God's order for submission? Why or why not?

_____

_____

5. *Have faith.* Read Daniel 3:8–10. The three Hebrew youth were convinced that no matter what happened to them physically, God was the spiritual victor. I am especially moved by their faith as they proclaimed in verses 17 and 18, "Our God whom we serve is able to deliver us from the burning fiery furnace, and he will deliver us out of thine hand, O king. But if not, be it known unto thee, O king, that we will not serve thy gods, nor worship the golden image which thou hast set up."

What faith! How is your faith when circumstances are good? Does it remain strong when you face adversity? Why or why not?

_____

_____

We can be victorious daily in Christ. It is not a matter of "letting go and letting God," but of purposefully dressing for battle each day.

REVIEW THE DAY

What was the most meaningful sentence or Bible verse in this section? Rephrase that particular sentence or verse as a prayer to God.

_____

_____

OUR RESPONSE—ONE DAY AT A TIME

What action does God want you to take as a result of today's study? Meditate, think deeply, and listen to your heart; then write about the action you will take.

_____

_____

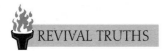

REVIVAL TRUTHS

- God provides a suit of armor for daily victory in battle.
- God also provides tools for our use in battle.
- God has already won any battle we daily face.

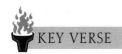

KEY VERSE

If it be so, our God whom we serve is able to deliver us from the burning fiery furnace, and he will deliver us out of thine hand, O king. (Daniel 3:17)

DAY FOUR

DAILY LIVING

The challenge today is to live the Gospel. Those who are without Christ will look at us and ask, "Can there be a God?" Good or bad, cliché or not, we are the Bible others read. Henry Blackaby, author of *Experiencing God*, has reminded Christians of a certain expectation: Darkness will act like it's supposed to—dark. That's its nature. The problem is with the light, in that too often you can't tell the believer from the unbeliever because the fruit is the same.

Of course, the question to us then is how should we live? Chuck Colson in his book *How Now Shall We Live?* maintained that in America we are embroiled in the latest culture war, the forces of evil against the forces of good.[3]

Jesus was concerned with daily life. Read the Beatitudes, Matthew 5:1–12. Don't skip over this familiar passage, but read it slowly, considering how each of these play out in daily life. Summarize the theme of these verses.

In those verses, the opening of the Lord's Sermon on the Mount, Jesus wasn't speaking to a group of religious leaders. He wasn't even speaking to the "church" as we know it today. He was speaking to average people looking to live according to God's plan. I have to believe that if Jesus talked about these issues, they are important for our lives.

What characteristics of His followers did Jesus mention in verses 3–11?

Consider your own life. Which of those characteristics are exemplified in your life?

_____

_____

Which ones seem impossible—or very, very difficult? Why?

_____

_____

God continues, even today, to honor the free-will choices we make. While He wants what is best for His children, He won't go further than we'll allow. Throughout this book we've discussed issues of spiritual growth that impact both personal revival and revival around the nation and the world. Brokenness. Repentance. Obedience. Prayer. Using your spiritual gifts. Evangelism.

In your daily life, how far do you want to go with God? He is the same today as He was with the Israelites in the desert. He offered manna for that day. It is no different now. He offers us the choice each day to determine how far we'll go in trusting Him, in serving Him, in loving Him.

> *As the deer panteth for the water,*
> *So my soul longeth after Thee.*
> *You alone are my heart's desire,*
> *And I long to worship Thee.*
>
> ———
>
> "AS THE DEER"/Martin Nystrom

A vivid picture is presented in Ezekiel 47:3–6. Read those verses now. The prophet of God is given a vision of living water with varying depths. The prophet is led into deeper and deeper water until is it so deep all he can do is swim. I believe that daily God wants to take us to deeper and deeper waters of relationship with Him. But He doesn't push. He leads. It's up to us to follow.

Where is God calling you to move deeper in relationship with Him? In obedience? In relationship with others?

_____

_____

Make a commitment and plan now to grow deeper in this area.

_____

_____

Being the Mississippi farm boy that I am, I understand about roots. I understand that if a plant doesn't have good roots, firmly grounded in well-watered and fertilized soil, the plant won't make it. It can't survive any harsh changes in weather. Even if it has an uneventful growing season, it won't produce much fruit. Isn't it wonderful the tangible examples God gives us to see how we should daily live? We are no different from a plant. We must have roots that grow deeply into the fertilized soil of God. If we don't reach down on a daily basis, we won't survive. At best, we'll be fruitless.

REVIEW THE DAY

Read Psalm 1:1–3. What are the characteristics of one daily rooted in God?

_____

_____

How does that apply to your own life?

_____

_____

Do you walk in the counsel of the wicked? How so? If you don't currently feel you do, how can you avoid doing so in the future?

_____

_____

Today make a fresh commitment to ask God to direct your life. Write a prayer with that commitment below.

_____

_____

What was the most meaningful sentence or Bible verse in this section? Rephrase that particular sentence or verse as a prayer to God.

_____

_____

_____

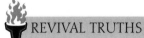

REVIVAL TRUTHS

- As believers, the fruit of our lives should be different from the unbelievers around us.
- Our lives serve as an open Bible to those around us.
- God calls us into a deeper relationship daily—if we'll go.

KEY VERSE

Blessed is the man that walketh not in the counsel of the ungodly, nor standeth in the way of sinners, nor sitteth in the seat of the scornful. But his delight is in the law of the Lord; and in his law doth he meditate day and night. And he shall be like a tree planted by the rivers of water, that bringeth forth his fruit in his season; his leaf also shall not wither; and whatsoever he doeth shall prosper. (Psalm 1:1–3)

DAY FIVE

DAILY JOY

Joy is an indicator of our spiritual state. In the Old Testament, joy is often connected with dancing, musical instruments, clapping, leaping, even foot-stamping. In the New Testament, it is associated with salvation, eating, drinking, or feasting. Joy is not an emotion. It's an outpouring of God's Spirit into action. It's a fruit of the Spirit, as seen in Galatians 5:22. It's impossible to experience joy without it showing. That was God's intention.

Paul often contrasted the concept of joy, even from suffering, with the boasting that humans do about themselves. Our joy comes from boasting in what Christ has done rather than in anything we even think we can accomplish on our own.

Joy from the Lord not only gives us strength, it *is* our strength. Nehemiah 8 describes the events after the rebuilding of Jerusalem's walls. Ezra came before the people to read the Law of Moses. As Ezra read, the people fell to the ground to worship the Lord, weeping as they listened to the words of the Law. There was recognition of the meaning of the Law, and the hearts of the people had ears to hear. Nehemiah exhorted the people to stop mourning. They were to gather choice food and share it with the poor. There was no room for grieving, "for the joy of the Lord is your strength" (verse 10). After this celebration of seven days, there was a time of confession from all the Israelites, and then a gathering of those chosen to live within the city walls.

Read Nehemiah 8 and notice the order of events. There is an understanding of the law and repentance. Then there is a great celebration of joy. Then a time of confession occurs, followed by a gathering into the city walls. This is not unlike the process of revival.

> *The highest and most desirable state of the soul is
> to praise God in celebration for being alive.*
>
> Luci Swindoll

God's law is made clear and people accept the atonement of Jesus with great joy. We continue on in confession, and also gather others into the kingdom of God. Joy is a cornerstone in the revival process.

What is your definition of joy?

_____

_____

How is joy expressed in your worship? In your daily life?

_____

_____

Just as fruit grows on a tree, the fruit of joy can be cultivated to grow in our lives. How? First, be led by the Spirit of God and not the Law. Second, run from acts of your sinful nature. As soon as you recognize something as sin, repent, confess, renounce, and run from it. Third, beware of pride and envy. Fourth, recognize that trials are intended to cause growth. Embrace them rather than lean away from them. Determine that you will treat them with joy rather than disgust, knowing that whatever evil is intended, God will use for good.

Finally, stay connected to the vine. Jesus promised that if we stay connected to Him, our joy will be complete. It will take daily discipline to grow in this area, but God is faithful.

Of the five steps listed above, which presents the most difficulty for you? Why?

_____

_____

Philippians 3:12 says, "Not that I have already attained, or am already perfected; but I press on, that I may lay hold of that for which Christ Jesus has also laid hold of me." If you take the hand of God and move one step along with Him, then

He will take you to the perfect places prepared for you, both here on this earth and in the world to come.

Revival begins in each heart. Revival ends in each heart. We have been given the joyful task of sharing the salvation of Christ with others, as we know it ourselves. That is what revival is all about. It flows from God, to the individual, to the world, and back to God.

Are you willing to go on this road? Are you willing to take His hand and walk with Him? Are you willing to allow Him to daily rekindle the fire He has placed within you? Be courageous. Walk in joy.

REVIEW THE DAY

I recall an old saying in Sunday school that perhaps you have heard too: JOY equals Jesus, Others, and You. That statement brought into perspective the process for growing the fruit of joy. We focus on Jesus first; He leads us to care for others, and in the process we are also cared for. We don't need to worry about ourselves when we are being cared for by the Creator of the universe.

Read Hebrews 12:2. Are you able to look to Jesus first? How does this affect your joy?

_____

_____

When you face trials, can you be joyful in the midst? Explain your answer.

_____

_____

What was the most meaningful sentence or Bible verse in this section? Rephrase that particular sentence or verse as a prayer to God.

_____

_____

_____

What action does God want you to take as a result of today's study? Meditate, think deeply, and listen to your heart; then write about the action you will take.

_____

_____

REVIVAL TRUTHS

- Joy is not an emotion.
- Joy is a result of His Spirit, an outpouring of the Spirit into action.
- We can experience joy by daily focusing on Christ.

KEY VERSE

My brethren, count it all joy when ye fall into divers temptation. (James 1:2)

LOOKING AHEAD

Hopefully you have discovered ways of relationship in Christ to rekindle your fire. Also, I hope you have discovered the joy in sharing that fire with others. Our God is a great God, who not only created us, but loves us enough to ask us to participate in spreading His kingdom.

Revival will come in America, one heart at a time.

# NOTES

Introduction

1. Henry T. Blackaby and Claude V. King, *Experiencing God* (Nashville: LifeWay Press, 1990), 15.

Chapter 1: A Life Ready for Revival

1. Richard J. Foster, *Celebration of Discipline* (San Francisco: HarperCollins, 1988), 7.

2. Jim Tomberline, sermon notes, Woodmen Valley Chapel Church, Colorado Springs, 28 February 1999.

3. Edward E. Plowman, "Religion News," *World Magazine*, 19 September 1998, 33.

Chapter 2: Spiritual Brokenness

1. Dale Schlafer, *A Revival Primer* (Denver: Promise Keepers, 1997), 9–10.

2. Joseph E, Leininger and Terry Whalen, *Lessons from the Pit* (Nashville: Broadman & Holman, 1999).

3. John C. Maxwell, "Accountability Questions," online at www.injoy.com.

4. Dan Hayes, *Fireseeds of Spiritual Awakening* (San Bernadino, Calif.: New Life Publishers, 1983), 51.

5. Roy Hession, *The Calvary Road* (London: Christian Literature Crusade, 1950), 28–29.

6. Adapted from the two-part article "Prodigal Nation" by Peter Marshall. See Peter Marshall, "Prodigal Nation–Part 1," *Washington Watch*, June 1998, 1, 5; and Peter Marshall, "Prodigal Nation–Part 2," *Washington Watch*, July 1998, 1.

7. Ian Murray, "Prayer and Revival," *Heart Cry! A Journal on Revival and Spiritual Awakening*, 5 (Spring 1998): 23.

8. A.T. Pierson, as quoted in "Promise Keepers" document, July 26, 1996.

NOTES

Chapter 3: The R Word

1. Mary Hutchinson, "When Mourning Turns to Joy," *Charisma*, February 2000, 49.

2. Mike MacIntosh, *The Tender Touch of God* (Eugene: Harvest House Publishers, 1996).

Chapter 4: Obedience

1. Mark Buntain, Life Center Church, Tacoma, Washington, Sunday morning service, winter 1988, personal notes of author.

2. Ibid.

3. Wesley Dewell, *Revival Fire* (Grand Rapids: Zondervan, 1995), 52.

4. Ibid., 82–83.

5. Elisabeth Elliott, *Through Gates of Splendor* (Old Tappan, N. J.: Spire, 1970), 13.

6. Ibid., 26.

Chapter 5: Prayer

1. E.M. Bounds, *Power Through Prayer* (Springdale, Pa.: Whitaker House, 1982), 90.

2. Kenneth L. Woodward, et al., "Talking to God, An Intimate Look at the Way We Pray." *Newsweek*, 6 January 1992, 39–44.

3. Evelyn Christenson, *A Time to Pray* (Eugene, Ore.: Harvest House, 1996), 181–185.

4. Wayne Jacobsen, *The Vineyard* (Eugene, Ore.: Harvest House,1992), 73.

5. Edward Plowman, "Citizen Jane," *World*, 29 January 2000, 21.

Chapter 6: Knowing God Better

1. John Peters, "The History of Revivals, Part 4," *Revival World Report*, September–October 1998, 13.

2. Ibid.

3. Andrew Murray, *Absolute Surrender* (Chicago: Moody, 1988), 52–53.

4. Brother Lawrence and Frank Laubach, *Practicing His Presence* (Beaumont, Tex.: The SeedSowers, 1973), xi–xii.

Chapter 7: Use Your Gifts for Christ

1. C. Peter Wagner, *Your Spiritual Gifts Can Help Your Church Grow* (Ventura, Calif.: Regal, 1994).

2. Sue Kline, "Sacred Work," *Discipleship Journal*, January 2000, 10.

Chapter 8: The Practical Results of Evangelism

1. Adapted from Mendell Taylor, *Exploring Evangelism* (Kansas City: Beacon Hill, 1964), 19.

2. Lewis Drummond, "Revival 101," class notes, Southern Baptist Theological Seminary, Louisville, fall semester 1971.

3. Charles G. Finney, *Lectures on Revivals and Religion* (New York: Revell, 1868), 15.

4. John Pollock, *Billy Graham* (New York: McGraw-Hill, 1966), 53.

5. David L. McKenna, *The Coming Great Awakening* (Downers Grove, Ill.: InterVarsity, 1990), 14–15, 72.

Chapter 9: A Key Time in Spiritual History

1. Bill Bright, keynote address, Christian Leaders Conference, 4 November 1998, Atlanta; personal notes.

2. *America's Great Revivals* (Minneapolis: Bethany House, 1970), 57.

3. Ibid., 169

4. The first five headlines are from *Joel News International*, an E-mail bulletin, 4 February 1999. A free subscription to this semiweekly bulletin can be obtained by sending an E-mail to hub@xc.org; include in the message the command: subscribe joel-news-international.

5. From *Imprimis*, March 1999, 5.

6. Edward E. Plowman, "Who Affirms What?" *World*, 19 September 1998, 33.

7. Mell Winger, "The Miracle of Almolonga," *Charisma*, September 1998, 67–70.

8. As quoted in "Coach Fired for Praying for the Team," *Joel News International*, 4 February 1999; from a correspondent's account that was first reported 10 November 1998.

9. George Gallup, informal gathering with CEOs of Christian agencies, at International Bible Society, Colorado Springs, 1995.

Chapter 10: God's Work in Our Nation

1. George Barna. "The State of the Church," pastors' seminar at Compassion International, Colorado Springs, September 1998.

2 "Finding God," *Newsweek*, 7 February 2000, 32–34; "Jesus of Nazareth," *Time*, 6 December 1999, 84–94; and "Dark Prophecies," *U.S. News & World Report*, 15 December 1997, 62–71.

3. Bill Bright, "Ready for Revival," *Worldwide Challenge*, July/August 1995, 4.

4. Byron Paulus, "Revival in the Nation—Hope for Hopeless Times," *Spirit of Revival*, 26, no. 1 (September 1996): 4.

5. Clay Renick, "Taking on the Taboo," *Today's Christian Woman*, January/February 1999, 46.

6. Ibid., 48.

7. Raymond McCaffy, "Devotion in Motion" *The* (Colorado Springs) *Gazette Telegraph*, 23 August 1998, A1.

8. Tom Pedigo, "America—A Christian Nation?" *American Family Association of Colorado* newsletter 2, no. 7 (July 1997): 1.

9. Carolyn Kleiner and Mary Lord, "The Cheating Game," *U.S. News & World Report*, 22 November 1999, 55.

10. CNN/*Time* poll, 20 August 1998, as reported on the CNN website; accessed June 21, 2000. Internet address: www.cnn.com/allpolitics/1998/08/20/adultery.poll/

11. James Garbarino, *Lost Boys* (New York: Free Press, 1999), 6–7.

12. "Publick Occurrences: The Week—The Fudge Factor," *World*, 16 May 1998, 8.

13. Ibid.

14. David Bryant, *The Hope at Hand* (Grand Rapids: Baker, 1996), 32–33.

15. Allan Bloom, *The Closing of the American Mind* (New York: Simon and Schuster, 1987), 82–83, 117–118.

Chapter 11: Vision for the World

1. Cal Thomas, "Cultural Danger Signs," *World*, 6 June 1998, 17.

2. Benazir Bhutto, *Daughter of Destiny* (New York: Simon & Schuster, 1990), as cited in Tom Phillips and Bob Norsworthy, *The World at Your Door* (Minneapolis: Bethany, 1997), 23.

3. Ibid.

4. Personal conversation with Charles Riggs, spring 1975, at the Greater Mississippi Billy Graham Crusade, Jackson, Mississippi.

NOTES

Chapter 12: Our Response—One Day at a Time

1. "A Letter to Our Community from the Parents of Cassie Rene Bernall," *The* (Littleton, Colo.) *Gazette*, 1 May 1999, 5.

2. Charlie Riggs, *Learning to Walk with God* (Minneapolis: World Wide Publications,1986), 64–70.

3. Chuck Colson, *How Now Shall We Live?* (Wheaton, Ill.: Tyndale, 1999), p. 2.

# RESOURCES

Chapter 7: Using Your Spiritual Gifts for Christ

Tim Blanchard, *Finding and Using Your Spiritual Gifts*, Wheaton, Ill.: Tyndale, 1979.

Don and Katie Fortune, *Discovering Your God-Given Gifts* (Grand Rapids: Chosen, 1987.

Dan Reiland, *Spiritual Gifts*, Atlanta: INJOY, Inc., 1998; www.injoy.com; 800-333-6506.

C. Peter Wagner, *Your Spiritual Gifts Can Help Your Church Grow*, Ventura: Regal, 1994.

Chapter 8: The Practical Results of Evangelism

Bill Bright, *A Handbook for Christian Maturity* (Ten Basic Steps Toward Christian Maturity Series), Orlando: New Life, 1994.

Discovering God Studies, Colorado Springs: International Students, 1998; 719-576-2700, www.isionline.org. The studies include four booklets: *Discovering God, Walking with God, Putting God First, and Sharing God.*

Growing Strong in God's Family, Colorado Springs: NavPress,1978. This is the new 2:7 discipleship series published by the Navigators.

Knowing God Personally, Colorado Springs: International Students, 1998.

Chapter 12: Our Response—One Day at a Time

Jim Logan, *Reclaiming Surrendered Ground* (Chicago: Moody, 1996).

RESOURCES

C. Peter Wagner, *Breaking Strongholds in Your City: How to Use Spiritual Mapping to Make Your Prayers More Strategic* (Ventura: Gospel Light, 1997).

C. Peter Wagner, *Warfare Prayer: How to Seek God's Power and Protection in the Battle to Build His Kingdom* (Ventura: Gospel Light, 1992).

MUSIC SOURCES